NATURE OF GOD

Exploring Creation to Meet the Creator

Jack Perkins

ISBN: 1514671425
ISBN 13: 9781514671429

A book from
Moosewood Editions
3916 Casey Key Rd, Nokomis, FL, 34275

Nature of God

Other books by author:

Parasols of Fern, Acadia Press
Acadia: Visions and Verse (Poetry and Photography)
Island Prayers: Photographs and Poems of Praise
Finding Moosewood, Finding God (Zondervan, Grand Rapids, MI.)
Marveling: Photographs and Poems of Praise

Dedicated as always to God
And His greatest gift to me
Mary Jo

The best remedy for those who are afraid,
lonely or unhappy is to go outside,
somewhere they can be quite alone
with the heavens, and nature, and God.

Anne Frank
Holocaust Victim

INTRODUCTION

Blame the years spent in television, reporting news. Consider, too, the years living on an island intimately immersed in nature, TV-guy-become-island man, gazing upon the glories of nature all around him every day, every night and beginning to think of those visions as — of all things – commercials!

Commercials for God.

Creation advertising its Creator.

Moved by that notion, the erstwhile reporter of news determinedly over years was transformed into a dedicated reporter of The Good News. Hence this book.

Not that I wasn't warned.

"Jack, a word of caution," counseled a wise friend, a longtime pastor, *"Don't even think of undertaking a book about nature and God –"* He paused significantly, smiled *"– unless you just can't help it."*

Dear old friend, dear new friends – I can't.

Not normally driven by impulse, I am driven by this. Nothing I have known fills me, nourishes and sustains me, nothing lifts me or is more important to me today than my God and the widespread advertisements for him we see all around us and call nature. God and nature.

I cannot *not* do this.

I've had a full life. A while back, I undertook to compile a list of things I had been able to do, permitted to do over the years – to either my pride or my ultimate shame. It ranged a gamut.

> Four decades of radio and TV; of wars; politics; elections; assassinations; murders and murder trials; petting whales off Baja California; winning Emmys; backpacking in and out of the Grand Canyon; singing with the Oak Ridge Boys; skiing the Olympic

downhill course (in two-and-a-half hours!); conduct-
ing the Boston Pops; narrating for the Boston Pops,
the National Symphony, the Venice Symphony; coach-
ing both sons' baseball teams; philosophizing with an
Idaho hermit named Buckskin Bill; photographing
with Ansel Adams; row-boating with Sophia Loren on
the *Bois de Boulogne*; graduating valedictorian from
cooks' school (OK - *Army* cook school); while in the
army, moonlighting as a disc jockey named Johnny
Morton ("That's the news, Morton reportin'"); breaking the Sam Sheppard murder case and it's "Trial of the
Century: scooping the world with the verdict; cursing
life's iniquities while watching slow death in the starvation camps of Africa; becoming a vegetarian; giving up
vegetarianism; preaching a sermon; hosting the Today
Show; guesting the Tonight show with Johnny Carson;
herding giraffe in Kenya with William Holden; smoking marijuana on a rooftop in Alaska where it was legal; inhaling another substance in a dismal Laotian
opium den; leaving my wife; returning to my wife a
week later; writing a song in Japanese for American
Olympics coverage; doing the only TV interview with
Sirhan Sirhan; having skin cancer, prostate cancer, and
kidney cancer; surviving all; investing in a Broadway
show; losing my investment in a Broadway show, and
having to pay for my own ticket to see it; dog-sledding
the Arctic slope; attending the wedding of the Shah of
Iran; being in-studio with David Brinkley on the assas-
sination of JFK; being run out of Jackson, MS by redneck moonshiners; being run out of St. Augustine FL
by redneck racists; broadcasting a commentary chas-
tising my own boss and winning an Emmy for it; learning the Rubik's Cube from Rubik; hosting New Year's
Eve broadcasts from Las Vegas; hosting Fourth of July

fireworks concerts from Boston's Esplanade; composing a musical; fighting a bull; nailing a child pornographer; being mistaken for Dr. Seuss; being mistaken for Marlin Perkins, being mistaken for the Frugal Gourmet; enduring logorrheic long distance calls from Marlon Brando; living in a Saigon apartment building all of whose other residents were prostitutes; giving witness on Robert Schuller's "Hour of Power"; broadcasting first film of Vietnam's Tet Offensive; being snowbound for two-and-a-half months in Maine; getting tear-gassed at a political convention; being tear gassed at *another* political convention; watching Evel Knievel beat my cameraman to the ground; getting revenge on Evel Knievel; years later, getting a contrite apology from Evel Knievel; having Frank Sinatra phone to say that he, Gregory Peck, Elizabeth Taylor and Cary Grant, dining together, had talked about what a great commentary I had delivered the night before; having President Lyndon Johnson, on another occasion, declare huffily, "I don't give a damn what Jack Perkins says"; growing network news' first beard and being required to shoot a Beard Screen Test so network brass could decide if I could keep it; having home destroyed by a hurricane where hurricanes aren't supposed to happen; being caricatured by Al Hirschfield and interviewed by Oprah; being impersonated on SNL and MST3K; doing television commercials for TWA (which shortly thereafter went bankrupt); doing commercials for State Farm Insurance (which, last I looked, was somehow still in business.)

All that and more, and you know what? Today, none of it – *none of it!* – means a thing.

What, then, the purpose of the list? Twofold:

1. To allow me to acknowledge with *gratitude* the years spangled with beauty and adventure.
2. To allow me to acknowledge with *guilt* ever being a man so filled with himself as to make a list.

That had to change. And it did with time, and the help of nature, God, and a small island.

In the northeastern United States, there is a species of tree properly classified as *acer pennsylvanicum,* also called Striped Maple, but most commonly known as Moosewood.

Also in that part of the country there used to stand a small cabin that my wife and I named Moosewood, a rustic island home that in its time helped remake my life. I wrote of that place and that transformative time in the book: *Finding Moosewood, Finding God.*

In this work, I invite readers to visit Moosewood again but, also, travel with me beyond Moosewood both temporally and geographically in a continuing pursuit of the God who pursues us.

God pursues us? That's how Christian writer Tim Keller put it: that while other religions posit a God whom people chase, hoping to catch with their good works and good words, rituals and rites, Christianity alone worships a god who comes *to* his people, pursuing. He came to Abraham instructing him to leave his homeland and, even at advanced age, make an arduous journey to a new land to do nothing less than found a new nation, new faith.

As God came to Abraham, he comes to his chosen ones today. (I used to shy from the appellation *Chosen Ones* but I shouldn't. It is not *I* saying that. It was Jesus himself, telling his disciples: *You did not choose me, but I chose you.*)

God comes by means of the Holy Spirit; he comes in the corporeal realization of his son, Jesus Christ; he makes himself known (to those would know) in the works of his hand all around.

St. Paul knew and told the Romans and, by extension, us:

What may be known about God is plain . . . because God has made it plain. . . For since the creation of the world God's invisible qualities—his eternal power and divine nature—have been clearly seen, being understood from what has been made.

Made plain through his works of nature.

Even before Paul, the Psalmist had written:

The heavens declare the glory of God; the skies proclaim the work of his hands. Day after day they pour forth speech; night after night they reveal knowledge . . .

That does not mean we should sit idly by, awaiting a lightning flash of sudden faith. Our pursuing God does not pursue out loud. It is a still small voice we are called upon to hear and heed; they are subtle signs we need attend.

Often, as Paul's letter and David's psalm instructed, they come through nature. It is through nature that we are captured and continually recaptured by our pursuing God. As this book's subtitle suggests, my purpose in exploring creation is always to meet the Creator.

I invite the Seeker to dip, unhurried, through these essays, writings that some will classify as nature writings which would mean bookstores would shelve them alongside great names of past and present – Thoreau, Abbey, Lopez, Dillard, Berry, Matthiessen, Muir, Teale, Leopold – this little book feeling a bit awkward and wholly humbled by the company.

The Library of America group published a worthy volume called *Environmental Writing Since Thoreau.* I know that *environmental* is a vogue and marketable word these days but far as I know Thoreau never felt need to use it and if I do it will be sparingly.

I won't use *ecology* at all. It has become too often misused by sloppy writers in the media (who usually don't even use the word *media* correctly as a *plural* noun.) *Ecology* is not a synonym for *environment.* The *-ology* ought to be the giveaway. It is the *study of* organisms and their environment.

Nor will I capitalize the word *nature*. Some people do (Thoreau did), as though believing that nature deserves that honorific. They either forget or refuse to acknowledge that nature is only the instrument used by God for adornment and instruction.

In my writing, the word "nature" is capitalized only if it starts a sentence or is the title. As for the title I have chosen for this book, *Nature of God,* I want quickly to assure the reader that that does not portend a dissertation on the character or characteristics of the Deity – I am not qualified for such exegesis. Rather, it is simply a way of ascribing the glories of what we hail as nature to their right and proper author. Many "nature writers" don't do that, don't choose to make any connection between nature and God. I cannot disconnect them.

The stories here are true. Or at least they are the truth as filtered through my own biased recall. I concede the bias. There's no escaping it. Would that everyone with bias and peddling tales would acknowledge it. There's nothing wrong with bias acknowledged. It's human. Bias unacknowledged corrupts discourse.

A while back I read a book written by a former colleague, a correspondent at NBC, Liz Trotta. I was especially interested in her recollection of things that happened when she and I were sharing a story here or there. I didn't remember them, or remember them that way. As far as I could recall, they had simply never happened. But that was as far as I could recall. I have never corrected her. Why should I? Why should I presume to deny her her version of events any more than I would deny any of you your memories of any of the tales I'm going to tell here even if they don't reconcile tidily with my versions. Hey, if you and I thought the same about everything there'd be no reason for both of us to be thinking.

A word about words. Mine have changed over years. When I escaped journalism some years back, (I consider myself now a "Recovering journalist"; one is never fully cured) I abandoned journalese. Too long I had spoken news-speak. I needed a new language as far from news-speak as possible.

I chose poetry. There are distinctions.

News fires at its quarry cannonades of language, using too many words to say too little; poetry distills.

News uses familiar terms – even clichés – so that people can comprehend without having to think; poetry wants people to think.

News is hurried and harried; poetry takes time to reflect.

News incites dispute and fulmination; poetry soothes.

News tells more than it knows; poetry knows more than it tells.

News endeavors to be as precise and unambiguous as possible; poetry delights in ambiguity.

The strident voice of news gets more attention than it deserves; soft-spoken poetry deserves more than it gets.

News is rarely worth reading; poetry is rarely read.

What is poetry? I think of it as an expression of the human desire to lift language, to raise it upward to that point where it finally dissipates as a risen fog leaving behind only the glow of exalted truth.

I also think of it as not a human invention. Poetry was created by the Creator, and that idea is not original with me. No less a thinker and teacher than C.S. Lewis wrote this in his book, *Reflections on the Psalms*:

> *It seems to me appropriate, almost inevitable, that when that great Imagination which in the beginning, for Its own delight and for the delight of men and angels . . . had invented and formed the whole world of Nature, submitted to express Itself in human speech, that speech should sometimes be poetry. For poetry too is a little incarnation, giving body to what had been before invisible and inaudible.*

There needs be wisdom in a poem but it need not be mine. Indeed, my wisdom is not sufficient. Oh, adequate for prose I think, and more than ample for journalism, but, aspiring higher, the poet must find a way quietly to plant a seed within his verse for the reader to discover, nourish and bring to bloom in the soil of God's gifted garden. It is a collaborative venture. The poet only sets down the poem; the reader writes it, the two of them bringing forth sprouted wisdom. Or at least whimsy. Or – if the air and the airs favor – both.

Air? Airs? Wordplay? Of course. If words are enlisted to do work for either a poet or a proseur, should they not be permitted also to play?

In that belief, poems whether playful or wise will be found disporting about in these pages, bouncing on the trampoline alongside nostalgic recollections, flinging Frisbees to sober contemplations.

Let the games begin.

BEING ENISLED

Yestermillennia, God appeared to man and woman on garden path, in bush afire, or capped with cloud on distant peak.

Today, He still appears though eyes to see Him be clouded, ears to hear Him, deaf. He still appears, observable to those who would observe, in every scintilla of nature surrounding.

For the Seeker, I commend an island. Let yourself be enisled, set apart on an island – littoral, literal or figurative. An island is a Petri dish in which more readily than abroad can be grown a healthy culture of awareness and appreciation of all creation. Which is to say, of God.

Island. Hear the music in the word. See the sunglints splashing from it. Savor the sweet allure. *Island.* Don't try to understand or attempt to explain. There is something inexpressible about islands.

The island on which my wife and I lived for thirteen years off the coast of Maine was in fact not simply an island; it was a "tied island," part of what is called a tombolo system, which sounds exotic though it means simply that there is a bar – in our case a gravel and mussel-shell shoal, that underlies the waters at high tide but is exposed at low tide, visibly connecting the island and the mainland. To complicate matters in this case, the "mainland" was itself a larger island – Mount Desert Island, MDI.

Geologic terminology and geographic quibble aside (how quickly they have distracted us from island magic) Mary Jo and I instantly, it seems looking back, became ardent and evangelical islomanes. British writer Lawrence Durrell had coined the term sixty years earlier, writing of a character in one of his books:

> *Somewhere among the notebooks of Gideon I once found a list of diseases as yet unclassified by medical science, and among these there occurred the word islomania, which was described as a rare but by no means unknown affliction of spirit. These are people, Gideon used to say, by way of explanation, who find islands somehow irresistible. We islomanes, says Gideon, are the direct descendants of the Atlanteans, and it is toward the lost Atlantis that our subconscious is drawn. This means that we find islands irresistible.*

To aspiring islomanes, islands seem to offer them refuge, escape and isolation and they believe they want those. They will likely learn that they don't want them at all. Plus which, islands don't provide them. Not really. What people try to escape by running to an island, they likely bring with them. The refuge they seek is from themselves. Isolation leaves them alone with what they tried to flee. For many, *Islands* is better as a magazine or a dream than a lifestyle.

For some though (us lost Atlanteans?) an island can be balm and devotion, a future that when it becomes present one prays will never be past.

We seek wonder. All, in our own ways and every day, hunger for wonder. The irony about wonder is that, though immense and immeasurable, it is best seen small. Try to magnify it, scrutinize and analyze it, and like a butterfly poised atop a black-eyed Susan, as you near, it flies. Look quickly. Wonder comes in glimpses.

Islands are made for glimpses. Limited themselves, they impose limits upon all who tread them. Not like mainlands where views and perplexities abound and minds overload. On islands, perspectives are bounded and within their harboring bounds a mind can finally focus on the boundless.

On the other hand, there is a deception to islands. Comprehensive, they pretend to be comprehensible, wanting you to think that what you can measure, you can assimilate. Able to walk the island from shore to shore and end to end, you assume that one day you can know it and hold it, complete, in the palm of your heart. But you can't. You can come closer to comprehending an island than a miasmic megalopolis or fractious federation but still you can't. And that's fine because believing that you can makes you try and the trying can be a worthy life-pursuit. In the end, an island's dissembling is another of its blessings.

It has to be small, the island of choice. Any bigger is not really an island. Geographers notwithstanding, Manhattan is not insular; Manhattan notwithstanding, "insular" is no insult.

What is it that attracts us to islands? Secularists and Darwinians may posit an atavistic impulse imprinted on the human organism to return to the bosom of the waters from which first wriggled its distant progenitors. That is a conceit believers don't believe.

Then what? Is it the echo of Crusoe, of the lore that deceives us twice: first assuring us that self-sufficiency is desirable, and then persuading us that it can be achieved?

Do we take an island as antidote for bigness?

Is it the quest for root in rock that sets us adrift?

All these questions bubble forth though their answers, alas, do not bubble with them. As Mary Jo and I found ourselves, surprisingly to both friends and ourselves, living on an island we knew only this: We had been seduced. And blessed. That small Maine island, by our choice, was ours; we, by God's choice were its.

Two thousand years ago, Paul of Tarsus exhorted the people of Thessalonica (and by extension, us) to "Rejoice always and pray without ceasing." Rejoice and pray. Islands are perfect for both.

As for rejoicing, in nature it seems easy and, well, natural. Absent the bristling bustle of big city, the paralyzing demands of urban conformity, one can better feel nature's pulse, sense her breath, hear her heartbeat and accept that her pulse and breath and heartbeat are those of God – nature's creator and ours.

As for praying, islands are symbols of our unbreakable tie with God. They themselves are tied, their tie at times made periodically visible as with our tombolo; at times, implied. As the island only hides but never loses its tie to the mainland, so the islander may seem to enjoy isolation in his insularity, but he too remains invisibly, inexorably connected. He has not escaped. He cannot fully loose the bonds.

The island, thus, is a metaphor both for the lives of its people and for its people's connection with God. God is our mainland. We may try to abscond, may think we have absconded, that, John Donne notwithstanding, man *can* be an island and we are. Tides flow and so dazzled are we by the waters that intervene that we forget what always underlies. Some of us are reluctant to acknowledge a connection to a God we cannot see and in whom we may believe that we do not believe, but, friends, listen to that bell buoy over by Sheep Porcupine island, it tolls for us, tolling the truth that through all, still and ever, we *are* connected. Even if we don't recognize it until the tide goes out. Or faith comes in.

Daily, we pray for that faith.

Our Maine island, a half-mile upthrust of granite, soil and woods, through history had worn other names, known other lives, welcomed other walkers through its flower-spattered meadow, ripened wild cherries for other eager mouths, spread sublime panoramas of sparkling seas as welcome reward to other climbers of its peak, but as we first found it, we knew none of this. Like most discoverers, we preferred to think our discovery unique, our experience unprecedented. But it wasn't. And as we understood that, we celebrated it, acknowledging that we were not there to be the story. The island was the story and deserved to be. The mindset with which one approaches an island is all-determining.

> *Don't come to an island to "find yourself,"*
> *Those who float that platitude*
> *Are chasers of bubbles, catchers of air.*
> *Forget the New Age attitude,*
> *You cannot find what is not there.*
>
> *Scrub off the makeup, discard the disguise,*
> *Lose the mocking costumes sewn*
> *For roles you need no longer play.*
> *Your lines were someone else's lies;*
> *Islands urge: Compose your own*
> *(And not what you think someone thinks you should say.)*
>
> *An island is not a place to pretend.*
> *Ring down the curtain, mute the applause;*
> *The time has come for the drama to end.*
> *No more cheers, no more huzzahs,*
> *Naked the player, naked the soul.*
> *Playing yourself is the hardest role*

Don't come to an island to *find* yourself but to *become* yourself. And to become yourself, it helps to know the past. Cicero:

> *To be ignorant of what happened before you were born is to be ever a child. For what is man's lifetime unless the memory of events is woven with those of earlier times?*

What were our island's earliest times? We sought to understand.

It was the age of fishes. Primeval seas teemed.

When was this? Scientists speak of the Pleistocene epoch of geologic time. And the Pliocene, Miocene, Oligocene, Eocene and Paleocene epochs. This was before those. Before the entire Cenozoic era, prior to the Cretaceous period, the Jurassic and Triassic periods of the Mesozoic era; pre-dating the Permian, Pennsylvanian and Mississippian periods – way back in that part of misty pre-history called the late Devonian period of the Paleozoic era – 375 million years ago – the elemental rock that would be our island was born.

(Please understand: I speak now in the terminology and time-scales of Geology not the Bible. So doing I do not mean to deny or affirm Biblical statements. I believe Science and Bible can be reconciled by reasonable people though that is not my purpose until a later chapter.)

We shouldn't call that proto-land I spoke of as North America because continents were still moving, floating about on the surface of molten earth. Probably the chunk we now think of as our continent had just collided with the crustal plate which would one day divide into Africa and Europe, the titanic collision crumpling our continent's fender so that suddenly (geologically speaking) there were mountains – the Appalachians – down whose flanks ran rivers which slowly, laboriously tumbled rocks into pebbles, ground pebbles into soil, carried soil back into shallow seas where it grew on sea bottoms as layers of silt, ever thicker, ever heavier, gravel and coarse sand, hundreds of feet thick, pushing down on itself with such pressure that it hardened once more into rock. And that rock, sedimentary and conglomerate, created on ancient seabeds so many millennia ago would one day be named by geologists the Bar Harbor series. The bedrock of our island.

The molten, moving earth still had tricks. Alternately, it began to rise and then subside and then rise and subside. What yesterday was sea bottom tomorrow was land. Then not. Continents wandered, riding their tectonic plates. Occasionally, globs of molten material from earth's deep furnace would force their way up toward the surface. Sometimes to erupt in volcanoes, sometimes to fracture the rock of the Bar Harbor series, squeeze through, around and over, and deposit layers of magma which would slowly cool into a hard rock called diorite. Other times, to push up, bubbling the crust and leave huge domes of another especially resistant rock called granite.

Erosion resumed. Soft rock was stripped away, leaving tough granite cores and less resilient rock that happened to be protected by hard caps of diorite. Resisting erosion, these constructions soon towered over surrounding land as mountains, or, when seas returned, as islands.

Such was our island, an up-folding of that sedimentary rock of the Bar Harbor series capped and protected by diorite.

It would take millions and millions of years. And only in the last million would earth unleash its latest trick: Ice. Four times, continental glaciers rumbled down over northern North America. The last began a hundred thousand years ago, reached its height eighteen thousand years ago. Ice a mile thick weighted what we call New England, covering the small island, scraping and scouring it, depressing it, pushing its head once more into the sea. When finally that last glacier retreated, melting away, it released so much water that sea levels on the depressed land rose 300 feet above the levels we know today. Half way up hillsides can be found remnants of beaches.

Again, seas subsided, land rebounded, and, again, there stood the island, its diorite cap upthrust from surrounding waters, the sedimentary rocks of its Bar Harbor series exposed on its flanks below that cap, while ocean waves slowly washed in to dump at the western end of the island an accretion of gravel that would form a bar to lie beneath the water when tides were high but run exposed when waters were low, a bar connecting the small island with the much larger granite island a third-mile away. And island off an island, tied together yet separate.

In that kinship, the small barren island existed for countless centuries. It basked in the sun, bore the waves, received the rains and the seeds delivered by birds. From the seeds sprouted plants. To feed on the plants came animals, insects, reptiles and more birds.

People?

As the island had come late to the face of the earth, people came late to the island. It was understandable: the only people anywhere on earth at that time were scarce scatterings of stone-age nomads who, having not yet discovered agriculture were still chipping out stone points to kill animals. This was the age before pottery, before metals, long before any sort of civilization, or alphabet, or numbers, or money. It would be four thousand years until Egyptians would build Pyramids; six thousand before the reign of King Solomon; seven thousand years before Jesus of Nazareth.

And nine thousand years before two seekers would take up residence on that small island, survey the glories of nature all around and praise the God who gave them both the glories and the senses with which to enjoy them and place them in poetic context.

In the beginning – what happened? – We are told
That God created, simply by saying the word
Land and sky and sun and plant and bird;
All the beauties abounding that we behold
He created, so we are told

In the beginning – what happened? – We're also told
That science in its wisdom has inferred
That these were not created; they occurred
A cosmic accident, quite uncontrolled
Created even us, so we are told.

Where lies the truth? Where lie the lies?
Should we trust the wisdom of the wise?
Or, as seeking, seeing islanders, believe our eyes?

Bar Island is a rare place on earth where the record of ages is not buried beneath soil or city but exposed. On the island's southeast face, cleaved meaningfully, are the tilted layers of siltstone, the Bar

Harbor series of 400 million years ago. See too the protective cap of diorite from the Devonian period, rock today popularly described as "unerodible." Scientists don't use that term or accept that anything is "unerodible." They ask us, instead, to look beneath our feet as we walk the rocky shore. Notice the yellow or black scabs on shore rocks, microscopic pairings of fungus and alga that appear to be harmlessly decorative but in fact are very, very slowly destructive. Acids released from those minuscule organisms will break down the minerals, leaving rock vulnerable to rains and waves before whose relentless batterings, ultimately it will succumb.

Other forces, too, conspire. There is disagreement on causes more than effects, but if our world undergoes a warming of climate – whatever the causes – that would mean that, obedient to laws of physics, warming waters will expand and seas rise. Scientists wonder if collapsing ice sheets might add waters, raising ocean levels even higher. They realize that northern North America, having rebounded from glaciations, today is subsiding once more with the rate of subsidence quickening. Land subsides, rock erodes, waters rise, scientists ponder and God alone knows the answers.

Will the island endure? Geologists talk epochs and eras. The rest of us think lifetimes. By human perspective, the rock that safeguards the island is unerodible enough. The island is eternal and our sweet, green memories of enlightening joy, everlasting.

We never met Eugenia Rodick though we came to know her well. She had grown up romping and frolicking across the meadows and woods of the same island that eighty years later we would think of as ours. She, too, had sweet, green memories of enlightening joy and, when grown, she undertook to set them down on a couple dozen pages of typescript which ended up moldering over in the basement of the Bar Harbor town library. Discovering them, my wife began working up a series of lovingly detailed pencil sketches reliving a girl's playful, thoughtful life where we now lived.

...Around the edges of the open grass plot were masses of peonies, tiger lilies, sweet William, phlox, lupine, columbine, bleeding heart, nasturtiums and, against the barn, there were the wild violets, a mass of the loveliest, long, thick-stemmed violets I have ever seen growing wild. There they were, year after year, and we nearly went mad picking them...The pasture was behind the big red barn near the swings and on Sundays the horses – Nancy, the gray mare work horse; Fencer, the driving horse which took us back and forth to town at low tide; Molly, my uncle's trotting horse; and Racquet, a quarter-horse which we used for our very own – stood with their heads on the pasture bars watching us at play ...next came the orchard where my Aunt, with the help of the hired men experimented with grafts on the old trees, getting her instruction from garden books – and her results from heaven!

... All along the steep southern bank of the island grew chokecherry bushes, lovely in the spring and fun to eat, to pucker up one's mouth in the early fall......at low tide here was an inexhaustible supply of clams to be dug along the shore ...

... Uncle Milt ran the fishing business on the shore. We were always on hand when the fish were running well and it was not unusual for the weirs to be so full that when the seine boats went in to gather the fish we would get out of the boat and wallow around on the solidly packed but live and squirming fish...

... Then there was the western point, a contrast to the boisterous eastern shore. Sometimes on summer evenings, our Aunt would suggest a walk to the point to see the sunset. A path led through the woods from the back of the house. There were bunchberries, blueberries, partridge berries, checker berries, twin sisters, wild lily of the valley, trillium and Indian pipe. But best of all, there were ferns of many kinds including wonderfully tall green bracken which we children used for parasols. We promenaded proudly beneath them, emerging finally from the woods to the rocky shore ... where, all unconsciously, we gave thanks for the glory and the peace and the benediction of a Maine sunset.

They were commonplace moments she lived but she put them in words and that made the difference. Her words are lenses that magnify the prosaic and render it rare. Children have that knack. Most adults forget to try.

Eugenia said she and her brothers gave thanks for each beautiful sunset. We gave thanks too, to God and to her – the One for providing the eventide miracle, the other for calling attention. Children have that knack too. Adults dismiss recalled moments of childhood as simplistic and saccharine. Why care?

Because – it is the child's sweet recollection that flavors the loving adult and adults who define the world. Want a more loving world? Recapture childhood's sweet truths.

It works two ways: Just as adults are here to teach children, children are here to remind adults. Bracken fronds as parasols? What a delightful image for a girl to conceive and a woman remember. It reminds us that the mind is kind. Memory clings to bliss and aggrandizes good while veiling the bitter and mean. That's not enough, of course. Selective memory can change only *then*. Many of us want to modify *now*.

Eugenia seemed to know how, seemed to understand that the mind's beneficent power works as well in present tense as past – that to alter lives we need to reframe attitudes; that as selective memory rewrites yesterday, selective perception can edit today. As we choose each day to dwell on the sublime in life, life will be sublime. Or, put another way:

Those fronds of green that spread at the foot of the oaks, if you think of them so, they are bracken – wild, inedible, useless. Or, if you wish, they can be parasols. On an island, you always have that choice.

And one way or another, we all live on islands.

SMALL

I told you that we named our island cabin *Moosewood* after a common tree of the area. I chose that because it was the tree I wanted to be.

The moosewood is an understory tree, feeling no need to be on top. Nor, after a long career of direct and reflected celebrity, did I. Moosewood is a small tree. I – at least in my mind – had been big for too long and wanted, now, to be small.

If wonder, as last chapter taught, is best seen small, perhaps it is true, also, that lives are best lived small. Smallness, though a given grace of islands, is attainable anywhere. There persists, however, confusion about it. The word is often used as a smear. *Small = Smear.* As in:

I hear it said our problem is we live our lives too small, trapped in a maze of the mundane, threading through puzzles of pettiness – alarm clocks and showers; shaves or makeup; morning tube-talk engulfing, asphyxiating us with the argumentative and insignificant as we bolt down breakfast or a shot of bottled wake-me-up, and dash to the car, train bus. Small. Gossip at work, small. Facebook, Twitter, friends and strangers wanting to think that we care what they are doing and thinking though we don't. Through all, serving as the dissonant accompaniment to our lives, a degenerate form of music that isn't, and lyrics that shouldn't be.

And the news, the ceaseless outbreaks of "breaking news." I hear it said there's so much breaking news because it's such a broken world. To escape the brokenness, or at least ignore it, people of small lives look down. They look down at the sidewalks they walk, look down to avoid seeing people, avoid invading another's space or permitting invasion of theirs. They look down at iPads, cell phones and newspapers disgorging news that itself is small. In the end, inescapably, that news and that gossip make small people look not just *down*, but *out*. Look out for all the dangers in their paranoiac world. Look out for themselves since no one else will. Look *out*. LifeLock can't lock a life. So *down* they look and *out* they look but all too rarely *up*.

We've been taught better. We have the counsel of St. Paul as he wrote to the believers in the city of Colossae. This is how Eugene Peterson's Bible, *The Message,* paraphrased it:

> *Don't shuffle along, eyes to the ground, absorbed with the things right in front of you. Look up, and be alert to what is going on around Christ—that's where the action is.*

Learning to be alert and aware, really seeing the things we see, hearing what we hear, not just observing but absorbing – that is our assignment, our duty and our blessing-in-waiting. And it too is small.

Poet Elizabeth Barrett Browning absorbed.

> *Earth's crammed with heaven,*
> *And every common bush afire with God;*
> *But only he who sees, takes off his shoes,*
> *The rest sit round and pluck blackberries . . .*

We plucked blackberries in Maine. What's more, our dog, our Australian Shepherd, plucked blackberries too. We first gave him the taste for berries by handing him samples on our walks up the late-summer lane toward the island meadow. He developed an appetite for those blackberries or raspberries depending on season and was soon adept at getting his own, plucking very carefully to get the berry without the thorns getting him. We named him for his new skill – Browser.

Is that story small?

We used to have a goat. Her name was Butterfly. This was when we lived in L.A., Butterfly, a Christmas present my wife asked for one year. Alas, Butterfly never did get the hang of suburban life, was never interested in mowing the grasses on our two acre hillside out back wishing instead she could be inside the house with the dogs and cats and us. The plate glass bowed dangerously when she stood on her hind legs as her front legs tried to knock politely if a bit too as-sertively on the sliding living room door. In other words, she shirked her assigned mowing duties and threatened the plate glass, all the while scattering random poop-pellets across the concrete deck which California breezes devilishly rolled into the pool. It had seemed a good idea. Maybe it would have worked had we had more patience. The morning after Christmas, Butterfly was back on the farm she had come from.

Is that story small?

The dogs and cats were family and like the rest us, arriving in Maine from California, had to adapt – to island living, to unaccustomed wildlife neighbors, and to weather far different than they had known. We could tell from tracks in the first snow where Tramp, California cat, had spied a red fox in his path and, wheeled about, to beat a bounding retreat to the safety of home. But we would never know what happened to him months later when he simply disappeared for three days, somewhere on the island (unless an eagle had snatched him off) but answering none of our anxious calls and we covered every foot of woods and meadow and peak and shore of the half mile long island which we and he and his feline and canine siblings pre-tended to control. Vanity is powerful in the new islander, though hu-mility must inevitably supplant it.

When Tramp finally came home, suddenly appearing outside the glass door one afternoon, he was grimy and glowering and reeking of musk. He must have escaped something (same fox?) and been holed up hiding somewhere for some time till he felt it was safe to crawl out and dash to safety with his people. Who hardly had a chance to hug him and pet him and express the appropriate sentiments before he wriggled away and bee-lined to first the water dish then the food. We would never know.

Those stories, I'm aware, are small.

For cats – we had two at the time – an island opened opportunities for hunting as well as being hunted. They learned quickly. Out in the meadow where tall summer grasses hid the tunnels of a myriad meadow mice, the cats learned both *how* to catch them and *which* to eat and which merely to take home as trophies. The voles, they learned, were fine dining. All that remained of those critters when a cat proudly deposited them on our doorstep were head perhaps and entrails. Shrews, on the other hand, they would kill and bring home – in either order – but never eat. There is a poison (to cats) about shrews and somehow our cats knew. It's true throughout the animal kingdom. Cattle learn to avoid the deadly hallucinogen, Jimsonweed, appropriately also called locoweed. Sometimes, yes, cattle *are* smarter than people.

For our hound dog, Buford, there was understandable puzzlement. He heard us *ooh* and *aah* over cats who brought home their trophy voles and shrews so why was it, one day when he went out hunting clear to the far end of the island as we could tell by the distant triumphant hound-howl, and returned to the cabin toting his proud catch, a full-grown, dead raccoon – why, he must have wondered, did we get mad and reprimand him. His expression – if one can read a dog's expression and I think its people can – said, *So what's with you people? Cats bring home trophies; you praise them. I bring home mine, you chew me out. You humans are impossible to figure.* His next trophy, days later, was the leg-bone of a deer. He never would tell us that story though it, too, was probably small.

But is that bad? Like most people, I used to think that to say someone was small, or lived a small life, or told small stories was degrading. The big, important people were the ones we honored and esteemed. People like people in *People*. It's the *big* who make things happen – at least according to the big who journal the happenings. The small may occasionally get a grudging millisecond of renown as curiosities – the citizen who rescues a kid from drowning in icy Tucker's pond, the waitress at Hank's Diner who comes over the counter to apply the Heimlich on a choking customer, or the small-town high school senior who aces the SAT's. Big moments but otherwise small people.

Those I have decided are my heroes; the small, my models; smallness, my intent.

I hear John Lennon singing of those who "want a revolution," acknowledging that "We all want to change the world," and I don't relate. I have never had world-changing aspirations, nor believed them feasible. I am small. I know I am small. And the things I aim for are small. First, before anything else, simply to know myself and then to have revealed to me God's plan for my life. A twist of Lennon:

> *I say I want a <u>revelation</u>*
> *Yeah, but ya know*
> *I <u>don't</u> <u>want</u> to change the world*

I may be involved now and then in un-small things, but never again should they be the measure of me. Let it not be said that I am not a small person contentedly living a conspicuously small life. To be a big person with a big life requires grandiosities and self-aggrandizement. Browser would not want to go berrying with a *big* me. Tramp would never come home. Buford would know that I would disdain his deer leg. Butterfly would recommend someone send *me* back to the goat farm, please, and have them *smallen that guy*.

In the small it is easier to discover the large. The smaller I am and know myself to be, the more room for God to fill my life. He is not a small God, else I would not find him everywhere I turn as now I do.

That tag of bark shed from the luminous trunk of a paper birch, on it I see what I fancy are hieroglyphs and hear the voice of one of his own reading to me of his grace.

I find hieroglyphs, too, on the sands of an island beach where tides, in their comings and goings, have left behind sand-ripples and curls which, to my small eyes are codes, even messages.

> *Could it be*
> *The hieroglyphs inscribed on morning sand*
> *Are God's encrypted rules,*
> *All that we need understand*
> *To live in concord,*
> *Please our Lord,*
> *Eschew disgrace and sin?*
> *Could it be?*
>
> *Decipher fast –*
> *The tide is coming in*

Some of my fondest friends I have never seen. Or if I have seen them at all the glimpse was but brief. And yet to this day I feel a bond with each in my remembering mind.

Summer in the northern woods. There is something inhabiting this place that I have never seen but love. It is small, seclusive, hermitic and yet of no little renown. Indeed, it was this fragile bit of life that our country's greatest early poet chose as his proxy in one of his greatest works. Walt Whitman's poem was an elegy for his beloved fallen leader, Abraham Lincoln. It was titled "*When Lilacs Last in the Door-Yard Bloom'd*" and, yes, dissectors of poetry, those desiccated dissectors who taught English in my high school and yours, have analyzed this poem to reveal the meaning of his mention of lilacs and other symbolism, concluding that when he spoke of the hermit thrush, he was speaking of the bard, the poet as himself mourning the death of Lincoln. I find spirituality in the thrush's song as well, reminder of rebirth made possible by a forgiving Father. As the melody of a liquid flute I hear the voice of the hermit thrush, adored but mostly unseen.

Winter, a crisp sun-bright morning that casts sharp shadows in the prints of my passing. Snow crunches with every footfall as I wander the meadow. Rising breath fogging my glasses renders a surreal softness, almost dreamlike quality to the morning tableau. In addition to hearing the sounds of my own passing I am keenly aware of other senses too: the pain pinching either side of the bridge of my nose – the curse a glasses wearer knows from metal frames in frigid climes; the prickly congesting of ice forming in nostrils; an ache in fingertips that would have been better clad in mittens this morning than gloves.

Still, all considered, I'd rather have tiny discomforts and be out here this morning than be home, warm by the wood stove. I don't know it yet – one never knows when it might happen – but I am about to make a new friend. One has to be flexible, willing to suspend both time and disbelief. I am willing.

By now I have made it most of the way to Pa Rock, the large, half-sunken boulder my wife's father, Pa, always liked to clamber up onto. He was short. It was aptly sized for his throne. By now it is cleanly clad with snow. I climb it and from that vantage look back at the way I have come, at the tracks I've been crunching into the snow. And I spot something I failed to notice on my way. Smaller than mine and crossing mine perpendicularly are other tracks. Dismounting, I walk back to study those tracks. My wife is the expert in our family on both animal tracks and animal scat. I take a guess which she, later, will affirm. They are indeed the tracks of the red fox. We've seen signs before but never have I come this close to meeting him. How close, I wonder, was it? Had he just come this way moments before my arrival and I had not been observant to spot his footprints? Is it possible – could it possibly be – that after I passed that point and paused to inventory my wintry senses, the glasses, nostrils, fingertips and all, that at that moment when I was looking ahead at Pa Rock, otherwise oblivious, that only then, behind my back he – or she (could be a vixen) – had scampered across my path and gone her way? Did she notice my tracks? Did she care? Was I, to her, a threat or an object of interest or of no concern whatever? Walking on, I come to an old stump and brush it off. Sitting there, I begin imagining, and in that surreal, soft-focus morning I convince myself that I had actually met her. (By now I had no doubt: she *was* a vixen.) Had met her and almost had conversation. The whole imagined encounter unrolling in my mind.

> *Today I took a walk in the meadow where she had taken a walk*
> *Our snow tracks crossed though just in space and not in time –*
> *This time*
> *But I have been this way before. It sometimes seems I stalk*
> *The lady. Not at all. Though I have come to know her well*
> *I've looked into her eyes and wished, while looking, I could climb*
> *Into her soul. I've wondered if it might not be*
> *That she, the while, was also looking, wishing, just like me*
> *I'd like to think beneath that rufous robe a friend might dwell*
> *Now, that's not realistic, the Cynic will deplore*
> *Ascribing human feelings to an animal that way*
> *I'm not ascribing, I'll reply, I'm wishing, nothing more*
> *A meadow walker's rueful dream that one bright snowy day*
> *That vixen, trotting through the meadow, my tracks here will see*
> *And maybe then – How lovely to hope! – She might think about me!*

Rising reluctantly from my snowy stump, I walk on. My glasses have cleared and there is so much to see. There at the brow of the hill leading down to the water is the rank of poplar trees – "popples" – their wood too soft to use for much but splendid for kindling on the morning fire. And over there, a cluster of other trees, small trees, gnarled and shrunken, even more-so here in the heart of winter, a foot of snow climbing their time-gutted trunks. These are all that survive of a homeowner's orchard a hundred years ago. In summer, the trees still do their best to make apples, but what meager fruit their old wood produces is dry and sour. Yet they try. They try. Their persistence alone is a lesson. And their shriveled fruit will not be wasted. My vixen will appreciate.

Back to the summer meadow, undulating in capricious breezes, keeping secrets of another world existing beneath those grasses in summer. A big-footed intruder who tromps overhead, if he sees anything, sees but clues — the miniature burrow holes twirled in the grasses, entrances to labyrinthine mazes constructed by some of nature's most fevered creatures, shrews and voles, meadow mice of such ferocious metabolism that almost each waking hour they must eat or perish. Rarely does Bigfoot see them. Pulled by his own mind-drift, caught in his own thought-web, he is usually oblivious to any world but his. He walks meadows, admires flowers, and ignores so much else. Summer, though, is an invitation to plop down on grasses — face up if one would take the Rorschach test of the clouds, face down to confirm the belief that heaven is under our feet as well as over our heads. Peering down, survey minuscule wonders: the nodding frailty of blue-eyed grass; the soft dark-green carpets which, closely inspected, are myriad tufts of hair-cap moss, their spore-capsules borne atop miniature pedicels, stately, small and usually overlooked. It is a common plant on our island. Its complexities are demeaned as common. *Polytrichum commune* is its Latin name. But how uncommon it is to gaze upon it here as it quietly, in its own small way, denies disbelievers and affirms its Creator.

It is His face I see in the secretive blossom of a violet. A single patch, a miniature bouquet of violets I find nestled in the grasses this afternoon by the big oak. They always nestle, violets, and almost always surprise. They weren't here yesterday as I came by, I'm sure of that. I would have noticed. I certainly would have noticed. But it rained through the night; the morning was drizzly, and then midday the sun broke through and now on this soft, green hillside – here they are! Are they harbingers? I pay my respects to these delicate forerunners. Seeing their sweet faces, their five petals, gentle traceries of tone on each, I think of the flowers' singular distinction, violets being the only flowers ever to have a color named *after them*. It's true, the flower was not named after an already categorized color, but the other way around. Way back in the 14th century, the purplish hue lying on the color wheel between red and blue, an admixture of both was named "violet" because it struck a whimsical taxonomist as the very color of the small flower he admired that was so named. Over years, the hue of this small flower became the mark of royalty and for western Christian churches the liturgical color of advent and Easter. This remarkable flower, what a treat to find them, this tiny nest of spring's precursors.

But, no, these are not simply forerunners. They are invitations to all who would see to look around. Up there on the hillside. See? Another tiny cluster, almost ignored, and past it, another and then another. The hillside, my eyes slowly become aware, is abundantly adorned with mini-bouquets of wild violets. Subtle, they are. Theirs is not a hue that commands. Their color may be regal but they do not parade as royalty. They, as we, are commoners.

And small.

Like my eyes.

I think about these flowers so small and my eyes so small and I thank God. Had my eyes been designed larger, with wider aspect, more like the photographer's 12 mm "fish-eye" lens focusing across a 180 degree sweep, how awful would that be. If I could apprehend broad vistas of nature's great glory in a single exposure, I think I might not be able to bear it. It would be too much for small me. Fish eye lenses are fine for fish. But for me there would be so much to see that I would not see it. Through a 12 mil lens, I would surely miss the nestling violets, miss seeing in them God's unseeable face.

I would miss them too in a big city. Miss much. Here, I must acknowledge a bias, a strong and confessed aversion to a metropolis, to say nothing of a megalopolis in which I had lived. To me, the word conurbation sounds like something that shouldn't be done in polite society.

For someone seeking smallness, it might seem paradoxically easy to accept yourself as small in a big city, tucked away in its high-rise warrens, rendered insignificant. But no, not insignificant at all, rather the city denizen is inclined to feel aggrandized by the boast-worthy awareness that you are an authentic Big Citian. You're not small. You're a New Yorker! An Angeleno! Nothing is small in Texas, we're told. Isn't Dallas called "Big D? " In big cities, no one is small. (Except *other* people.)

Which brings me to what I will forthrightly label as:

A Small Man's Rant!

Big cities are like cigarettes: people know they are hazardous to health but still get hooked. Back in the early 1600's, England's King James I, turning his attention from the new Bible he had commissioned to a product recently introduced to genteel English society, scathingly denounced tobacco as "loathsome to the eye, hateful to the nose, harmful to the brain, dangerous to the lungs, and in the black, stinking fume thereof nearest resembling the horrible Stygian smoke of the pit that is bottomless." Apt description for smoking. Four hundred years later it fits cities. With foul air and polluted manners, they poison. With congestion, cacophony and angst, they infect. With swaggering self-importance, they presume to intimidate but in fact merely bore. With jangling frenzy, they file away nerve-ends. (It was city-dweller Gore Vidal who wrote "It's not enough to succeed. Others must fail." He was joking?) City sidewalks are gauntlets, challenging you to pass by the pitiable poor without pitying, to exercise either apathy or disgust, neither a wholesome attitude.

Morality in big cities is aberrant. Should and shouldn't are not operative constraints, only can and can't. What happened to manners? She writes a syndicated column. Where are courtesy and politeness? Missing persons. In New York, the fable said, when a man stood up in the subway to offer his seat to a lady, she fainted with surprise. Revived, she accepted the seat and thanked him — and he fainted. One day in New York, fighting a noontime intersection, I stepped back to allow a woman to cross in front of me and she stopped, fixing me with a bemused gaze to say, "You're not from here, are you?" Courtesy, said the cynic, is that form of polite behavior practiced by civilized people when they have time. In cities, they don't have time. Was Emerson right, that "the end of the human race will be that it will eventually die of civilization?"

Still, as tobacco companies deny the evils they purvey, so cities have fervent apologists. Defending miasmic metropolises, they shrug off discourtesies and filth, speaking instead of energy and excitement; lauding cultural diversity, they say things like "there's always something to do." Take such people to the country and they'll moan about "nothing to do." Like smokers trying to quit, they need something to do with their hands, something to do with their time, something to do. Could it be that the person who so desperately needs something to do really needs something to be?

Again, I am not arguing that others should uproot and relocate simply because so many big cities are execrable. I think they are but others don't agree. Still others agree but are willing to accept city distress in fair exchange, so they feel, for some perceived benefits. So be it. But for me, then and still, big cities are repugnant. Nature appeals. Creation appeals. The Creator appeals.

(End of Small Man's Rant!)

THOREAU

When my book, *Finding Moosewood, Finding God* was published, some of the reviewers were so profligate with praise as to compare it to the works of Henry David Thoreau. One went so far as to headline his piece: *Jack Perkins Writes a Walden For Today.*

As a man with my fair ration of pride, I was flattered. At first. But then I got thinking. To be sure, readers enticed by such reviews might be motivated to buy the book and, as I considered it in so many ways the most important work I had ever done, I lusted for its widest distribution. On the other hand, I am sharply aware that Thoreau and I – to put it plain – have a great deal in *un*common!

Some things we share, of course, but on balance ours would be a contentious and challenging friendship if timing and circumstance permitted it to be. (Actually I once did a television interview with him. Sort of. I'll tell you.)

I know I have learned from Thoreau. Many have and do, although his simple instruction to *simplify, simplify, simplify* is today more recognized than heeded; his assessment that the mass of men lead lives of quiet desperation mainly makes us wonder – was there ever a time when desperation was *quiet*, not the helter-skelter brand that explodes our world these days?

He called himself a philosopher. That is not a trade listed on census forms today any more than there's a checkbox for "Prophet." Are there today no more philosophers or prophets? A young man who gets his degree in Philosophy, what is there for him to do but to teach Philosophy to other students who themselves won't find a professional place? The young woman who deems herself a prophet, won't people take her to be a palm-reading, crystal ball charlatan? Perhaps it's just that today we use a new vocabulary. Who used to declare themselves philosophers aggrandize themselves on TV now as experts and analysts and write *deep-think* books. Prophets are those in public life whose predictions have short half-lives and pollsters who ask "What do you think . . .?" to too many pollees who don't.

Cynicism aside, maybe there *are* still prophets and philosophers of biblical stature. If God once spoke to his people through the writings of Moses and David Solomon, Isaiah, and Jeremiah as well as those we demean today as the *minor* prophets in Old Testament days, and the apostles and epistle writers in New Testament times, did He thereafter fall silent? Had He nothing more to tell us? No more guidance? Had He said it all?

I once had the arrogant notion of putting together a New Bible, convening in its pages a contemporary Council of Nicaea to select what additional writings – philosophy, history, exposition and exegesis – might be meet for inclusion. What writings from the years between 325 A.D. and now. Are there any? I thought, of course of Augustine of Hippo, his *Confessions*. Thought of Martin Luther's 95 Theses, which may or may not have been nailed to that door of the Wittenberg church. In later years, John Calvin, John Wesley, and then C.S. Lewis and Oswald Chambers. M. Scott Peck, Rick Warren? Whom to include? Who to decide whom to include?

Thoreau had his own mind in such matters. He called himself a philosopher but was also a brilliant young aphorist and it was that talent that ensured that his philosophy was never obscure and ponderous but pithy. Today, many writers of philosophy emulate the obscurity; few, the pith.

Among the few pith-enabled was my favorite essayist, that evangelist for clarity and concision, E.B. White, who once wrote a delightful piece about purchasing a pocket copy of Thoreau's *Walden,* reading it, re-reading it, dipping into it so frequently that it began to take over his conversations. If someone asked his advice on living, he would parrot Thoreau's "Simplify. . ." (or fancy he had done so; he was never quite sure what had truly happened and what he had imagined.) A friend would ask why he hadn't been around lately and he would gently reply "If a man does not keep pace with his companions, perhaps it is because he hears a different drummer."

White was not alone in his admiration. Thoreauvian aphorisms are still as commonly deployed across society as Biblical or Shakespearean apothegms. Those people unfamiliar with Thoreau's writings are poorer for it. Those who know of but disregard his wisdom are probably too busy basking in what they consider their own.

When I paddled over to town next time, on my list was to see if the good folks at Sherman's bookstore would order for me the sixteen volume paperback set of Thoreau's writings. I, too, wished "to live deliberately, to front only the essential facts of life, and see if I could not learn what it had to teach, and not, when I came to die, discover that I had not lived."

Thoreau moved to Walden on July 4th, 1845; Mary Jo and I celebrated our Independence July 4th, 1986, by setting off for new lives at our Maine cabin, Moosewood.

He stayed at Walden two years and two months; we stayed at Moosewood thirteen years.

He lived in a cabin he built; we lived in a cabin we had built for us.

Thoreau, though living in heralded solitude at Walden, often left – walking the mile-and-a-half into town to keep up with friends and receive communications; we, some days, left our solitude at low tide to walk across the gravel and mussel shell bar a mile into town for mail and visits.

He liked to carry back from town one of his mom's fresh-baked pies; we backpacked groceries from Don's Shop'n'Save (in winter bearing them across the island by sled.)

While seemingly secluded, he had frequent visitors to his pond-side cabin, noted citizens of town come to witness his strange life for themselves; we, secluded on our island, had few intentional visitors though frequent accidental ones. A young couple, come to the island one night to do a bit of "sparking" (I prefer the old word over contemporary synonyms), got stranded when the tide turned and they couldn't get back across to go back to their dorms (both of them summertime servers at the Park's Jordan Pond House restaurant.) Sheepishly, they tapped at our bedroom window at 2 a.m. requesting only a blanket against the nighttime chill. Instead, we directed them to our small, separate guest cabin at the edge of the woods to spend the night and we'd see them in the morning. At which time, even more sheepish than the night before, they found awaiting them a hearty hot breakfast of coffee, bacon, blueberry pancakes and maple syrup, the only condition being that they never tell anyone about it. No use encouraging other sparking strandees.

Thoreau grew beans and potatoes; we tried to grow potatoes but after our first crop, local deer got wise and devoured our future intentions.

He became so familiar with the creatures around him that at his beckoning whistle a couple of crows would set down at his doorstep; we were asked by park rangers to take in a wounded crow that needed cage rest to heal a gunshot wing, whereupon Mary Jo dutifully and lovingly spent the next three months nursing it back to health and mobility.

Thoreau would walk the woods, exploring and noting observations, feelings and thoughts in a simple journal book; we would walk the woods, exploring and noting observations, feelings and thoughts back at the cabin on a laptop suckled by solar panels.

He didn't stay home – during the two years and two months he was purportedly in residence at Walden, he was often gone making speeches, junketing to northern Maine for what would be another book, even spending a protest night in the Concord jail; we visited family in Florida, traveled to do a bit of television and the closest I came to being arrested was getting a ticket for speeding while trying to beat the tide and get home. (The local officer understood and wrote fast.)

Thoreau preferred autobiography to fiction, saying of a writer, "We do not wish to know how his imaginary hero, but how he, the actual hero, lived from day to day"; I had once written a fictional thriller that had neither satisfied nor succeeded, so now, deciding that for me, in this regard at least, Thoreau was right, I kept my journal.

He cautioned readers to "Beware of any enterprise that requires new clothes and not, rather, a new wearer of clothes"; arriving at Moosewood after 35 years in broadcast news, I quickly ditched my TV clothes and hauled out jeans and sweatshirts.

Before he began his brief internship at Walden, Thoreau had spoken at Harvard commencement services, suggesting that, "The order of things should be somewhat reversed – the seventh should be a man's day of toil . . . and the other six the sabbath of the affections and the soul, in which to range this wide-spread garden, and drink in the soft influences and sublime revelations of Nature." That's how we lived.

He noted that it cost him nothing for curtains because "I have no gazers to shut out but the sun and the moon"; We disdained curtains for that reason and also because we did not want to miss the flashing colors at the feeders festooning our trees and deck, nor the warming light on the mountains of Acadia across the bay.

Thoreau spoke of a friend as being "not penurious but merely simple . . . not poor for he does not want riches"; when we made our leap from settled to unsettled lives, salaried to sanative, we did not know if we were being financially prudent. Our accountant back in California cautioned us before we left that he wasn't confident we could really afford to do this. Yet leap we did, assured in our own minds that somehow it would work. We would not be poor because we did not want riches.

Thoreau wrote that, indeed, "None is so poor that he need sit on a pumpkin," and for Walden he borrowed some of the furniture for his cabin and made the rest; we had no pumpkins available, so I made our dining room table and benches, our four poster bed, chest of drawers and a few windsor-style chairs from splendid replica kits, while Mary Jo crafted mirror frames, towel racks, and from fallen pages of birch bark, glued-up distinctive waste baskets and lampshades. Our coffee table was an old sled on runners, its top holding copies of *Mother Earth News, Smithsonian,* and *National Geographic* (No *Time, Newsweek* or *TV Guide.)*

Those were some of the similarities I noted between Thoreau's life and ours. But, as I said, there were also some sharply etched differences.

Thoreau spoke of the Bible as "an old book" of no greater worth to him than the writings of any other religion; for me, the Bible was unique and invaluable – the Book of Books, irreplaceable.

He wrote cynically about miracles: "Men talk about Bible miracles because there are no miracles in their lives;" He *wrote* of miracles, I *believed* in them, recognizing many miracles that had steered and continued to steer my life repeatedly and felicitously.

Many authors before him had written of the divinity of man, the divine residing within people. Thoreau's mentor and landlord, Emerson, had affirmed "I am part or particle of God." But of that notion, Thoreau sniffed: *Talk of a divinity in man! Look at the teamster on the highway, wending to market by day or night ; does any divinity stir within him? His highest duty to fodder and water his horses! ... How godlike, how immortal, is he?*; Sorry, H. D., I'm with Emerson.

Thoreau disparaged charity, calling it "the interference of a third person." He wrote "If I knew for a certainty that a man was coming to my house with the conscious design of doing me good, I should run for my life ... for fear that I should get some of his good done to me – some of its virus mingled with my blood." Belittling do-gooders, he wrote "A man is not a good man because he will feed me if I should be starving or warm me if I should be freezing, or pull me out a ditch if I should ever fall into one. I can find you a Newfoundland dog that will do as much."

In Maine, I got involved in several *Do-good* causes. There was "Friends of Acadia," a citizens group I helped found to support Acadia national park with fund-raising and trail building, and ultimately creating *pro bono* new videos for the park's visitor center. And there was the MDI Sheltered Workshops, a charity providing care, job-training and housing for developmentally challenged adults. It was through that group that I met a dear woman named Myrtle McCloud. For a long time, hers had been a harrowing life of being abused and then institutionalized. Only in recent years had she emerged from that hell to a proudly productive life thanks to the *Do-Gooders* of the MDI Sheltered Workshops. Now, her assigned and cheerfully fulfilled work was to superintend a local church where most any day you visited you saw her smiling face beaming a welcome bright as the sun pouring through a stained glass window.

Such worthy, charitable causes came to my mind – as did Thoreau's nagging cynicism – each time I went to the Bar Harbor dump.

There I had met Jim Rich, Jimmy Rich, the longtime attendant at the dump, guiding traffic, clearing spilled debris, telling folks what went in which container or compactor. He was tall, slender, usually unshaven, grizzled and gaunt. His clothes suited the place; if not fashionable they were serviceable – this was a dump not a men's store. Getting to know him if just a bit in visits over many years, we assumed he was not a man of means. But then he, too, it appeared, did not lust for wealth.

He had one personal side-job while working at the dump: on his own, he gathered spent bottles from incoming trash. He put them aside and welcomed it when visitors were kind enough to have already separated them from their refuse for him. Collecting them was a way for him to make a few extra dollars, we assumed, to provide for his family beyond what must be his meager town wage. We were glad to help, to "do good", Thoreau or no.

What surprised us when we finally learned the truth was that the used bottles he gathered were, in fact, part of a three-layer *Do Good* cake. We saved them for Jimmy at the dump; he gathered them to turn in for cash, yes, but not to benefit his own family. Rather, he donated his proceeds from those bottles collected – all the proceeds – to the MDI Sheltered Workshops.

Jimmy was Rich.

Another point of contention I had with Thoreau was this: denigrating news and news tellers, he wrote "All news, as it is called, is gossip and they who edit or read it are old women over their tea." Forget his denigration of newspeople, he did not honor older citizens; At fifty-two, roughly twice his Walden age, I *was* one.

He didn't beat around the mulberry bush in his disrespect for elders, writing: "I have yet to hear a single syllable of valuable or even earnest advice from my seniors. They have told me nothing, and probably cannot tell me anything to the purpose."

Writing: "Age is no better, hardly so well, qualified for an instructor as youth, for it has not profited so much as it has lost."

Writing: ". . . the old have no very important advice to give the young, their own experience has been so partial, and their lives have been such miserable failures . . "

He was sour and harsh in his ageism. This, in spite of the fact that his great friend and benefactor, Ralph Waldo Emerson on whose land he was squatting was already in his forties, would live to seventy-eight. Did Emerson have "no very important advice to give the young?" Was his life such a "miserable failure? Had he never spoken "a single syllable of valuable or even earnest advice" to Thoreau. One might have wondered: would Thoreau's own old age, when it came, mellow his attitude toward the old? One would never know. He died at 44.

On one significant matter it's hard to say whether I agreed with Thoreau or not because – by the evidence of his writings and the testimony of townspeople – *he* didn't agree with *himself*.

He wrote disparagingly of people who desperately frequent the local post office. "The poor fellow who walks away with the greatest number of letters, proud of his extensive correspondence has not heard from himself this long while." He boasted that "For my part, I could easily do without the post office. I think that there are very few important communications made through it."

However his fellow townsmen said that nobody went to the local post office more urgently than Thoreau.

There were dichotomies in the man. Deceptions or self-deceptions.

I once wrote a mock television interview program, hoping to interest PBS stations to use it to spin off a series of conversations I would do with famous figures of the past using their actual quotes. The series would be titled "In Their Own Words." The audition episode I wrote had me interviewing Thoreau, his responses all taken verbatim from his writings. The show never got picked up, partly because at about that same time, Steve Allen began a series like it and even more elaborate: roundtable conversations with groups of disparate but always engaging figures from history. I pursued my project no further. Recently, though, I came across a couple of stray pages from that original script with Thoreau. The subject had turned to his disdain of journalism.

The modern, cheap and fertile press. The adventurous student will always study classics.

Which many disregard for being too old.

We might as well omit to study nature because she is old.

And dull?

It is not all books that are as dull as their readers.

A man will go out of his way to pick up a silver dollar but here are golden words which the wisest men of antiquity have uttered and whose worth the wise of every succeeding age have assured us of. And yet ... We are illiterate. I do not make any broad distinction between the illiterateness of my townsman who cannot read at all and the illiterateness of him who has learned to read only what is for children and feeble intellects. We are a race of tit-men, and soar but little higher in our intellectual flights than the columns of the daily papers.

And the daily papers you don't think well of?

I have no time to read newspapers.

Isn't it important to keep up?

If you chance to live and move and have your being in that thin stratum in which the events which make the news transpire . . .

Thin?

Thinner than the paper on which it is printed – then these things will fill the world for you. But if you soar above or dive below that plane, you cannot remember nor be reminded of these.

A lot of people are; a lot of people do.

(THOREAU AGREEING) Hardly a man takes a half-hour's nap after dinner but when he wakes he holds up his head and asks, "What's the news?" as if the rest of mankind had stood his sentinels. Some give direction to be waked every half-hour, doubtless for no other purpose.

But not you?

I am sure that I never read any memorable news in a newspaper. If we read of one man robbed or murdered or killed by accident, or one cow run over on the western railroad, or one mad dog killed, or one lot of grasshoppers in the winter, we never need read of another. One is enough. If you are acquainted with the principle, what to you care for a myriad instances?

Let me pursue this just a bit further, Mr. Thoreau. Aside from the two years you lived here at Walden, you were mostly in Concord. At that time, didn't you want to know what was happening around you?

The news of the street? I am astonished to observe how willing men are to lumber their minds with such rubbish, to permit idle rumors and incidents of the most insignificant kind to intrude on ground which should be sacred to thought. Shall the mind be a public arena where the affairs of the street are discussed? Or shall it be a quarter of heaven itself, consecrated to the service of the gods?

Think of admitting a single case of the criminal court into our thoughts, to stalk profanely through their sanctum sanctorum. Would it not be intellectual and moral suicide?

You didn't want to know about such things?

It is so hard to forget what it is worse than useless to remember. If I am to be a thoroughfare, I prefer that it be of mountain-brooks and not town sewers.

So don't read newspapers?

Read not the Times. Read the eternities.

So he said. But what Thoreau *said* was not what Thoreau *did*. He may not have "read the Times," but he devoured the *Tribune*. When that New York paper was delivered, Thoreau was all over it. So reported various townsfolk, that hardly anyone in all of Concord read newspapers more eagerly than did the somewhat hypocritical Henry Thoreau. (Or if calling him hypocritical courts the enmity of ardent Thoreauvians, should I temper my language and remark merely his "equivocation"? Now and then, he himself seemed to address it. "I am startled," he wrote, "when I consider how little I am actually concerned about the things I write in my journal.")

Mary Jo and I read the Times. The *Bar Harbor Times* was the local weekly and usually that was the only paper we read. I was newsed out from working in the business for thirty-five years. Given our new lives on a small island, our whole appreciation of news was turned upside down. For us anymore, the important news was not in the papers but all around us.

It was in the leaves of the trees budding out in spring, shading us in summer, donning their assigned colors of flame in fall.

It was the doe proudly displaying her delicately spotted fawn at the edge of the woods, then the two of them, white flags flying, bounding away.

It was the sound of a thousand wings as a raft of eider on the waters off the island anticipated our approach with velvet applause.

It was the arrival from Arctic realms of an uncommon flock of redpolls flashing at our wintertime feeders, our shivering clime their retreat, their Florida.

It was the eagle from his nest on the next island swooping over to ours to alight on the old oak up from the shore, scouting for his dinner and then, having procured it, returning to his oak perch for a leisurely dinner.

It was Bruckner letting us know that a fog had blown in, Bruckner being our name for the lighthouse out on Egg Rock at the harbor entrance, its dolorous call, *Wooo-wah-wawoo, Wooo-wah-wawoo,* echoing the horns that open Anton Bruckner's Fourth symphony.

It was the unmelodic horn of the Bluenose ferry approaching the end of our island as it returned to Bar Harbor from its trip to Yarmouth, Nova Scotia.

It was the bouquet of smells rising daily to our cabin – the pungent iodine of seaweed exposed at low tide, diesel fumes from lobster boats cranking up to get their horny-handed lobstermen and stern men out to their traps by sunrise, the legal opening of the day's harvest. (Never on Sunday, though. A law lobstermen applauded forbade their hauling traps on the Sabbath).

It was the perfume of the boughs of balsam fir we snipped and bundled back to the house, pile after pile, to our sunroom transformed for the season into Jo's winter workshop, where over coming days, her fingers growing raw and sticky with resin, she produced several dozen fragrant Christmas wreaths to send off to less fortunate friends removed from natural Christmas aromas. Those little stuffed, fir-scented pillows from L.L.Bean just don't do it.

For us, these were the news of the day – any day – more important, more richly rewarding than whatever the *New York Times* might be printing that day.

(We relished the story told in Maine about a man named Tom Perkins. No relative of mine, he was a state legislator and also proprietor of a drug store in the small down of Blue Hill along the coast from us. Seems one day he was confronted by a visitor, a proper if haughty woman "from away" as Mainers put it, demanding to know why his little store did not have a copy of the Sunday *New York Times*. "I can't believe you don't carry *The Times*," she sniffed. To which he replied calmly, "Well, ya know, funny 'bout that, but I was down to New York a while back and went into a newsstand and they didn't have the *Blue Hill Packet*.")

Newspapers all bear heavy loads of advertisements, burdens that, in fact, some readers spend more time perusing than they do the news.

Of course, the news we received on our island through the nature that surrounded us was also full of advertising. On every page there were ads, some small almost unnoticed; some large, double-truck spreads, all of them advertising the same thing – their creator. Our Creator.

Those ads we thirstily imbibed.

GLACIAL ERRATIC

One of those ads leads me to a rock, a rock I like to climb and sit atop. A boulder, I should say to give it its due. Eight or ten foot diameter, mostly tumbled round but with one side slightly flattened so that as the boulder is positioned that flattened face creates a steep ramp to the top inviting me in T-shirt, shorts and sneakers to scale it. And did I mention that the boulder sits by the edge of the water, the edge of the sea, making its invitation irresistible?

From its top, I look down from my princely perch with a feeling of separation, of exaltation. Don't we yearn for that, the feeling of being exalted, lifted above? Of course those truly exalted (Mother Teresa comes to mind) are exalted by abasing themselves. Still, the urge is strong to be on top looking down even if it's only eight or ten feet down. The view is different, the perspective and sense different. From atop my rock I look down on where I would have been had I not been exalted. That's the quiet, contemplative joy. It's not that I feel closer to heaven up here, closer to God. It's not that at all. I do not honor the human conceit of a heaven up there in what I see as softening sky. I believe that the construct of a heaven residing above us – though frequently so depicted in the Bible – is a pleasant allegory, but an allegory.

How inspiring the spires that people
Of faith erect when a town they found
Building a church and lifting a steeple
To beckon the faithful from far around

Both steeple and their hearts they raise
While letting hearty voices fly
To fling their alleluia praise
Up toward the pastel-ribboned sky

Up to that gleaming if I'll-defined place
They allegorize that heaven must be
(Though they know it's merely astral space
Stretching incomprehensibly)

And thus, in a word, is the puzzle defined
"Incomprehensibility"
Mortal men of mini-mind
Unable to grasp what they cannot see

And so they conjecture a heaven place
To which one day they hope to repair
And meet their Maker face to face
Somewhere, could it be up there?

From my boulder-throne I do not look up to find heaven or find God for as I don't believe heaven is up there neither do I believe that our God is up there any more than he is down here. Down here beside me on my boulder. Right here, indwelling.

It's not an original thought. Back in 1741, the most popular evangelist of the colonies which would become America was George Whitefield. He preached The Great Awakening and when he talked about the Kingdom of God he spoke of how it can be found. Or *not*. He said it cannot be found by being of a particular sect or denomination, not by being baptized by water but never the Holy Ghost, not by simply knowing the language, being conversant with words like *grace* and *sanctification* and *justification.* All these, he said, are precious truths "but then I am persuaded that there are many who talk of these truths, who preach up these truths, and yet at the same time never, never felt the power of these truths upon their hearts."

Their hearts. That, Whitefield preached, was the answer not to where the Kingdom of God *is* located but to where it *should be.*

"Open the door of your heart," this renowned evangelist told American colonists, "that the King of glory, the blessed Jesus, may come in and erect His kingdom in your soul."

That, for us today, is the alarming, the damning truth. The Kingdom of God does not and cannot exist unless and until we give it a place.

Since ancient days, people have harbored a passionate need to place God. Greeks and Romans situated their deities on mountaintops; Hindus found their multiple gods at times residing in idols, temples, rivers, and animals; Buddhists acknowledged no god. For ancient Hebrews, God was said in the book of Exodus to have given specific instructions that a special place, an ark, be constructed "of acacia wood—two and a half cubits long, a cubit and a half wide, and a cubit and a half high. Overlay it with pure gold, both inside and out, and make a gold molding around it. Cast four gold rings for it and fasten them to its four feet, with two rings on one side and two rings on the other." Make this tabernacle, God told his people and "I will dwell among them."

In the Bible, both testaments are filled with references to heaven. The term "heaven and earth" became the way of meaning "everything, everywhere." As Moses led the Hebrews through the desert toward the promised land God provided for them by raining down "manna from heaven" as sustenance.

The prayer Jesus taught his disciples, that formulation that became known as The Lord's Prayer, began before anything else by placing God.

Our Father which art in heaven . . .

The English poet Robert Browning had a character speak what would become the famous expression of relief and consolation: "God's in his heaven; all's right with the world."

If there is a God, as much of mankind has long assumed, and as I avow, he has to *be* somewhere, in some *place*, doesn't he? Everything else we know is in a place, isn't it?

No. What about love? It's not in *a place*. What about inspiration and goodness. These aren't in *places*. And isn't God himself all three – love and inspiration and goodness? So why does he need to be in *a place*.

It can get quite pedantic, this line of thinking, even syllogistic. A few years back John Morreall, doctor of philosophy and professor of religious studies at The College of William and Mary wrote a disquisition titled: *Is God in Heaven?* He acknowledged that both the Christian Apostles Creed and Nicene Creed say that Jesus ascended into heaven and is now seated at the right hand of the Father.

But those were composed at a time Christians thought of their God as a physical being. Once the tendency was to consider God as nonphysical then the argument for God in a place called heaven was moot. As Dr. Morreall put the matter syllogistically:

1. Heaven is a place
2. Only what is physical is located in a place
3. God is not physical
4. Therefore God is not located in a place and, thus, is not in heaven.

Dr. Morreall wrote of Greek philosophy, of its concept of metaphysical dualism, the belief that there were both a physical world related to the body and a nonphysical world of the mind, spirit and soul. Writers of the Bible did not have this concept of dualism so felt the need to describe God as a physical being with hands and feet and walking about in the Garden of Eden. That's how they thought, how their limited understanding had them believing. They were primitive, those Fathers of our faith. The Spirit that moved them, that guided their hands as they set down what we would know as the writings of The Bible shaped their thoughts and words to be understood by the people of those times with their limited (by our standards) abilities to comprehend.

Why am I carrying on about this? Why, sitting here in T-shirt and shorts on top of a rock, am I pondering imponderables? Is there some mystical power to this rock? I know there are mystical and mystifying powers to other rocks. I have visited some of those, notably, the curious sliding rocks of Death Valley.

What photographers' dreams they are, many times photographed even if they are a challenge to get to. Winding and thumping for miles along a gravel road between mountains up in the northwestern corner of California's Death Valley, I eventually find myself looking out across the amazing phenomenon. There sprawls a long, flat stretch of desert sand more than two miles long, a mile or so wide and perfectly level. The elevation at one end was carefully measured by scientific instruments and compared to the other end two miles away. There was no more than an inch-and-a-half difference. The area is spoken of as The Runway, not because it's sandy flat surface appears as though it could be an airfield but because, in fact, it is. It is a runway for rocks. Though most of the *playa* is barren and bare, there are some rocks here and there, mostly squarish rocks weighing anywhere up to a couple hundred pounds. And they move. The photograph I make as so many before me have made is of a rock stationary on the wind-patterned sand surface and, trailing behind it, a clearly marked skid mark where that rock has traveled to get to this temporary resting spot. Maybe hundreds of yards the rock has slid across the sand and I can see the track distinctly but what I cannot see – or know – is *how*. What moved that rock? And all the others that make the same mysterious migration over time? You never see them moving. No one has ever seen the rocks moving, though move they assuredly and conspicuously do.

There are theories. NASA sent a team of observers to study the phenomenon and they generated many theories – winds tunneled between mountains able to move rocks when there's been just enough rain to cause a slick of mud on the sand's surface; occasional forma- tion of ice that facilitates the slides; animals? (That one doesn't work; there are never found animal tracks.) – many theories, no proofs. I like that. It's good to have natural mysteries to remind us that we don't know everything – or need to.

What does this have to do with me and my pulpit rock on the coast of Maine? This rock doesn't move, does it? Well, not lately, but if I sometimes feel I don't belong here perched atop this rock-throne, I remember that *it* doesn't belong here either. Not on this shore, not by this sea, not anywhere near here. Like me, it is from somewhere else, brought to this place by forces it did not understand.

It is like Plymouth Rock. Or boulders scattered with seeming purpose about New York's Central Park. It was the renowned land- scape artist, Frederick Law Olmsted, who most recently positioned those boulders around that Park. The original Positioner, how- ever, was nature and that's the story my boulder-throne makes me recall.

They are called glacial erratics, "erratic" coming from the Latin *errare* meaning to wander and oh, these rocks have wandered. Geologists can tell by studying their composition that there is noth- ing like them in these parts. Clearly, they have wandered here from somewhere else. In the case of Plymouth Rock which stands at the shore of Massachusetts and is said to have welcomed the Pilgrims in 1620 (though, in fact, those weary travelers had first landed on the tip of Cape Cod) that rock, too, is a new arrival, geologically speak- ing. This whole stretch of the American continent was transfigured by stretches of glaciation – one after another, ice sheets forcing their way down from the north, covering the land with crushing ice as much as a mile thick, and then melting, retreating, only to keep re- turning and retreating for tens of thousands of years. And each time they came, they brought with them rocks and debris which, once here, they randomly deposited and left behind. One of those glacial erratics became venerated by Americans, a curiosity remarked by no less than that perceptive Frenchman, Alexis De Tocqueville:

"Here is a stone which the feet of a few outcasts pressed for an instant; and the stone becomes famous; it is treasured by a great nation; its very dust is shared as a relic." Although no one is even sure which rock it was on which the Pilgrims landed.

And the rocks in Central Park? Olmsted, the landscape artist who designed the park, discovered those erratics capriciously scattered across the scape and had some of them moved to where he wanted them. *National Geographic* ran a photograph of a child scrambling to the top of one of those rocks and it reminded me so much of the rock on my own seashore and the man-child who loved to scramble to the top of it. That rock too was a glacial erratic like several other over in Acadia, the national park on the next island. Rangers took people to see them and lectured on these geologic anomalies. Especially one:

Bubble Rock
"Glacial erratic," the ranger calls it
Brought here by forces it can't comprehend
Delivered to this mountaintop
Deposited on perilous perch
To balance here
Equivocal
Unstable
Perhaps to plunge in the very next instant
(Isn't that always possible?)
Or perhaps accorded grace
To stay for yet a while
How long?
It does not know nor need to know
A rock brings its many yesterdays
Only as far as today
Existing in now
A symbol of solid uncertainty

"Glacial erratic," the ranger calls it
And I think: "So am I."

Is my rock a miracle? Are the sliding rocks in Death Valley? Am I? Do I hear answers from the reader or mocking? Then let me ask this: Do you, reader, believe in miracles? If your answer to that is no, answer this: With *what* do you not believe? With your mind? Aah, think about that. Isn't your mind itself is a miracle? (And if our minds do not think of themselves as miracles is it not simply because we have them burdened with so many unmiraculous thoughts.)

Some people, deifying artificial intelligence, think of computers as miracles. But just one small part of the brain, that which controls human vision, must perform up to 100 billion computations per second. How many of today's most powerful computers must be lashed together to equal that? Just asking.

So, if the mind is a miracle and a miracle, as sometimes defined, is the product of not natural but supernatural causes, then are we implying here a functioning deity? My cagy answer is this: The unconscious portion of the mind does not have to ask that question. The unconscious not only knows the reality of a functioning deity but, in ways which are vital for us to understand, is connected to it.

Meet the unconscious. Freud gave us the concept. Others, a half century earlier, had formulated it, but it was Freud who developed and popularized it. Within the mind's topography, he posited, are three precincts, three levels, three states of being, three processes (however they be best envisioned.) First is the conscious, comprising those thoughts and images we are aware of; second, the preconscious, holding things like a phone number which isn't instantly "on my mind" but can more or less readily be summoned; and third, the unconscious, that mysterious realm that lies beyond awareness, making itself known only subtly, through signals wafted upward in the form of dreams, fantasies, even what we call "Freudian" slips of the tongue. These signals, he felt, are more frequent than we acknowledge, and eminently more important.

His concept of the unconscious would later be refined by his colleagues and successors and it will be appropriate later in these pages to explore those refinements — vital matters like how to address more of the unconscious' potential, and whence the unconscious derives, that is, what it ultimately represents, all pertinent questions. For now, though, even before examining its genealogy, let us complete the cursory introductions.

Many of us call it "the subconscious." Or ignore the unconscious altogether, failing to understand its power and significance. Or if we appreciate its power, we appreciate it but vaguely. Consider some vernacular phrases. Asked how they shape their lives, determine their courses, some seemingly languid people say they "just go with the flow." Or "take things as they come." Sounds like rudderless life. Others talk of succeeding by "being in the right place at the right time." The word "serendipity" became a vogue word, people loosening it to tell of those turnings of fate that somehow, beyond their power, (so they thought), worked out well. I, for too long, credited "flukes." I had got where I was, I would say, through a series of "flukes." Not planned, striven-for achievements but accidents, coincidences, happenstances. So I thought.

Sometimes, mistakenly, you challenge the fluke and the feeling. The middle aged man experiences that cliche which sociologists and supermarket flimsies delight in describing, that itching to leave home and wife for no good reason except that he's never done it. But on the night he chooses to tell her, requiring extreme inebriation to do it, he finds himself in mid-declaration interrupting to go inside to refuel and while walking from backyard to house, in his stupor, walks straight into the swimming pool. Shallow end. Whereupon, pretending a dignity which in fact was relinquished much earlier, he sloshes across the pool with stately, slow-motion strides and steps out the other side as though nothing happened. Wasn't that a fluke, that bizarre image of himself haughtily hiking the pool which would torture his mind in days to come till he aborted his fancied escape and went back where he belonged. Flukes take flight, flukes fly home.

You come to count on it. Over years, I had come to expect that if I followed the undefined instincts that pointed and nudged, life would move and change and most always for the better. Experience persuaded me to trust. I had read Nehru's line: "Life is like a game of cards. The hand that is dealt you represents determinism; the way you play it is free will." Was I a determinist? Fatalist? I didn't think in those terms. Believing that something unerringly guided me but abashed by religion, too busy thinking of myself to think of a God, uncomfortable with notions of Freud or psychic powers, I chose simply to call things flukes.

That may sound like false modesty. It wasn't. It was real modesty. It was false realism. I did not credit the real forces at work in my life. Isn't that true of many, all those who talk about "going with the flow," or "taking things as they come," or "being in the right place at the right time," or blessed with "serendipity" or following "flukes?" Aren't they all — aren't we all — talking about the same thing but failing to give it its name?

It is the unconscious. (And perhaps even that doesn't give it its ultimate name; to that thought, too, we must return.) What we need learn to trust is not "flow" or "things" but the guidance of our own unconscious minds.

Not to claim that the unconscious controls external happenings, an occurrence like an auto accident, but it does determine how the mind processes the externals, chooses to react to them, the echoes which are awakened, the energies educed. How does this happen?

Freud's protege, Jung, coined the phrase: "The wisdom of the unconscious." In ways that were mysterious in his time and are hardly less so today, the unconscious selects certain impulses, images, kernels of ideas to send bubbling up toward the surface, toward the conscious. Perhaps as dreams, perhaps as fugitive wisps that appear and as quickly recede in the murky moments between sleep and waking. Perhaps as a thought occurring "from out of the blue" while we, composing, are in need of precisely that thought. Perhaps as a long-ago memory which floats up to blend with a current perception and jog us to a needed decision. Perhaps it is a warming sense of familiar comfort which a place we have never seen seems to evoke. We don't know why; we can't understand *deja vu*. The messages sent by the unconscious are powerful but subtle.

Do we receive them? That is the question. Some people block them out. If their unconscious is transmitting, their conscious hasn't switched on its receiver. Or else something — ego, the distractions of busy lives, doubt, or fear — scrambles the signal. In such unreceptive people, the membrane between unconscious and conscious seems impermeable. It ought to be Gore-tex, like a modern parka, the miracle fabric comprising billions of microscopic pores so tiny that lashing rains cannot pass through but large enough that water vapor, rising from the body, can. That's what the mind needs to demarcate its precincts, a membrane impermeable to the lashing of assumed guilts and repressed iniquities, ppthe pelting of worldly diversions (the quiet core of our being should be spared Hip Hop!), but permeable in the other direction to the vapors of inspiration which the unconscious wafts upward.

There is a charming irony to the unconscious. When it begins sending its signals, starts to short-circuit habits, supplant behaviors, subdue accustomed rationality, we usually don't realize what's happening. Our conscious minds don't discern the origin of the impulses. But here is the irony: the unconscious does. Conspiring with itself, it goads us into honoring its own intimations, whatever we choose to call them.

I called them flukes, felt they were blessings that befell me unbidden. Today, I believe that was wrong. More, I believe such an attitude is dangerous. We need to examine that matter but to do so, permit me the long way around.

Decades ago Freud reported that "About a third of my cases are suffering from no clinically definable neurosis, but from the senselessness and emptiness of their lives. This can be described as the general neurosis of our time."

Ours too. People carp and curse that someone else is "getting away with something," and pity themselves that they are not. They harbor anger and *angst*, fears and loathings. How poignantly they must identify on reading the first line of Dr. M. Scott Peck's pivotal book, *A Road Less Travelled*. "Life is difficult." Strong hook for a book, but on reading that line the first time, it took me aback. I stared at it. The book had come so highly recommended and that's how it started? With what, for me, seemed a patent untruth? Life, difficult? At the bottom of the page a footnote reminded that one of the Buddha's "Four Noble Truths" was the corollary that "Life is suffering." Also stunning; also, I didn't believe. Whereupon, as though addressing my qualms, the author proffered the following paradox: "Once we truly know that life is difficult . . . then life is no longer difficult." I pondered. I had never acknowledged that life was difficult, so why was life, for me, not difficult? Impatiently, I laid the conundrum aside, gratified that my life — for whatever reasons — had been bountifully blessed. I, we, had always felt that. Hearing advice columnists and pop psychologists proclaim that marriage is hard work, we shook our heads. Ours was not. Did that mean we had a special marriage, or special acceptance?

Or was it endorphins? Sociologists like to talk about those. Released in the body's normal bio-chemical process, endorphins had been found to be more powerful than synthetic opiates like morphine, in producing sensations of well-being. Exercise was said to stimulate the body's production of endorphins, affording an internal, natural, biochemical high. Perhaps Jo and I, perhaps others in life who seemed more accepting, adaptable, fundamentally satisfied – Shiners rather than Whiners – simply had more endorphins.

Whatever the cause, it was not surprising one day to hear Mary Jo say "I wonder why we're so lucky to have all this?" Were we unique? We found few echoes in books. Not in Sinclair Lewis' *Babbitt*: "I've never done anything I wanted to in my life." Not in Lord Byron: "I have not had ten happy days." Not in Simone de Beauvoir: "I have been gypped by life." How sad that people could feel that way.

Gail Sheehy studied women and men of well-being in her work *Passages* but found that "Repeated to a striking degree in the histories of the most-satisfied adults was a history of a troubled period during late childhood or adolescence, when many rated themselves as very unhappy. Some hit close to rock bottom . . . [with at least one] weak, failed, alcoholic, sickly or absent parent." Definitely not us. We had never had to work through torments, did not now suffer them. Our lives had been and remained so serene and congenial that — I hesitate to confess it — I was almost scared. There was a foolish, dogging fear that I never talked about and never acknowledged, but once, on a story, I met a man who shared it.

Dick Van Patten had been an actor and performer since childhood, always working, always in demand. He had married an actress, had a rich family life, enjoyed every day and wanted for virtually nothing. Now, in his fifties, he harbored an awful anxiety. Things had gone so well in his life that surely, to balance things out, horrible things were in store. A religious man, devout Roman Catholic, he wondered if the torments of Job would be settled upon him, some lingering blight to darken the last half of his life as joy and success had illumined the first. In the New Testament he could read Luke's account of Jesus warning the multitudes: "Woe to you who are rich, for you have received your consolation. Woe to you who are full, for you shall hunger. Woe to you who laugh now, for you shall mourn and weep." Didn't those words of his Savior justify his fear?

Psychologists talk about the Impostor Phenomenon. Some successful people, believing their success to be undeserved, fear it must be only a matter of time before the world discovers them as impostors. (Of course, the opposite of believing your success is not deserved is believing it is, and that carries risks of its own.)

What Dick Van Patten felt was not the Impostor Phenomenon but something akin. Let's call it the Symmetry Syndrome, the quirky, illogical assumption that life will mete out, if not always justice, at least symmetry. That all your happiness today augurs terrible times coming tomorrow. The reasoning is utterly unfounded, but, in a perverse way, ineluctable

Again, false modesty is not the problem. The problem here is real modesty, overdone. Dick Van Patten was an extraordinarily modest and self-effacing man. In the public eye that can be a problem. You go through life acutely aware of people studying you, perhaps wondering if you're another stuck-up show biz guy, asking themselves why does that lucky buck get to "have it all." So fearful are you that that's what people are thinking, you begin to wonder if they're right. There lies the danger. Whether in public life or not, if you accept the fiction that "it all" was simply handed to you, to undeserving you, you risk the Symmetry Syndrome.

To allay this anxiety, one must recognize that the quality of life does *not* depend upon flukes. Know that life's patterns derive from an interworking of circumstances, the impulses of the unconscious, and consequent actions. That last is critical. To match serendipities there must be bold, positive action. Contrary to the popular expression, you don't fall into good fortune; you make a decision and jump. You'll never see the glorious panorama from the top of the mountain till you climb it. To "go with the flow" — you must *go*.

Give yourself credit. Acknowledge the flukes, the good breaks that come, and accept them, but only as bases upon which you must build. A whale knows: a fluke gets you nowhere until you power it.

Or put it another way. Back in the "I-I" sixties, comedian Flip Wilson attired as his alter ego in dress and high heels, he would shrilly proclaim: "What You See is What You Get!" The line caught on and, in the lassitudinous seventies, became a popular slogan, a resigned way of saying "Hey, that's life." In the high-tech eighties, computerists, saving bytes, compressed it to its acronym — "WYSIWYG" — pronounced "Wissy-wig" — meaning a computer program that let you see on the screen precisely how a document would look when printed. Well, computerists can keep it, but the rest of us should dispose of the line. As philosophy, it never was more than a psychic shrug — *Take it or leave it* — the philosophy of a person willing merely to *follow flukes.* Dynamic life, self-determinative life, demands better than philosophy from a comic in drag. Here is a better rewriting: What you see seize is what you get.

Filled with a spirit I'm not really certain I have, I scamper down from my throne-rock and set off on this new day to *seize.*

BLISS IN THE DESERT

I am Ecclesiastes.

Long I have quested for happiness and gratification only to find that, once achieved, those were meaningless, vanity, smoke. Try harder, I thought. Push further. Others seem to be finding satisfaction and happiness, don't they? But then, like the earlier Ecclesiastes, I finally came to understand that even when found, those were not enough. Happiness was empty. Satisfaction didn't satisfy. I recalibrated. Henceforth, I decided, whatever I might claim to be seeking as I roamed through life, my ultimate goal would be bliss. Not simple jocularity though I do enjoy wit. Not frivolity, for frivoling is surely meaningless, vanity, smoke. No, at their heart (and in mine) my peregrinations henceforth would be the gentle but purposeful searching for bliss.

Let not the word be mistaken. These days, the word bliss appears in many guises, presenting itself variously as a candy, a comic strip, a magazine, a skin lotion, a boutique in Knoxville, a restaurant in Philadelphia, a cupcake bakery in Oregon, a "Gentlemen's Club" in Florida, a Texas military base, a singing group, a movie, and, of course, we are told, the equivalent of ignorance.

Those aren't the bliss I seek.

The word has a distinguished pedigree dating back to the Old English of a millennium past. *Perfect happiness, great joy, a state of spiritual blessedness.* Yes, semanticists acknowledge a connection between "blessedness" and "bliss."

Hippies in the Haight in their days of drugs spoke of getting "blissed out," meaning rendered oblivious to everything else. Nor is that the bliss for which I quest. I want not oblivion but its opposite – awareness, acute awareness, profound understanding and the bliss that comes from those.

Mirth, hilarity, gaiety, frivolity, merriment – those are feelings of the moment, a guffaw at a joke, the tickling enjoyment of an entertainment, reactions to external stimuli. Bliss, on the other hand, grows not from *without* but from *within.* Hilarity is a flash of lightning; bliss, moonlight. A mirthful person laughs; a blissful person smiles. Gaiety wants others to share, is heightened by social excitement; bliss glows alone. Uproarious people bellow their music; the blissful hum to themselves. Frivolity springs from dining, dancing, traveling, shopping, partying. Bliss needs none of those. It is not a result of doing, but a way of being.

Fulton Sheen talked about bliss. Remember the Archbishop Fulton J. Sheen? If you are too young, be assured and perhaps astonished to learn that indeed there once was a time when a major television network in America would broadcast a program — and in prime time, yet — that was nothing but a Catholic priest standing before a theater audience each week with no TelePrompTer, no cue cards or notes, just standing by a blackboard with a little toy angel sitting on top, the priest talking gently and sincerely about goodness and God-ness. This was in 1951 and the network he was on, DuMont, was more renowned for programs of merry mirth like Jackie Gleason's "Cavalcade of Stars," or the wacky hilarity of Ernie Kovacs. But those never got the audience Archbishop Sheen commanded. Nor were they named Personality of the Year by the Emmys as he was.

Though slotted in a "suicide" time up against "Uncle Miltie," Milton Berle, and on another network, Frank Sinatra, when Sheen's weekly chalk talk began threatening the big guys' ratings, Berle was heard to crack, mirthfully, "He uses old material too." Which got jolly folks joking that Sheen should be called "uncle Fultie." Eventually, Sheen's show, "Life Is Worth Living," was drawing as many as thirty million viewers! Today, in a country with twice as many people and five times as many TV sets, a hit show, scripted and very expensive, is thrilled with an audience a third of what Sheen attracted every week. But then shows today don't have what the good Monsignor had sixty years ago: *bliss.*

He spoke of it one evening, making a point that a teenaged viewer in Ohio would never forget. Bliss, he said, is both a condition and a practice. Yes, he acknowledged, the word blissful means "full of bliss," but it also implies "promoting or inducing bliss." You have it, you spread it. Archbishop Sheen embodied bliss; he spread bliss. Since him, TV has pretty much settled for mirth. As do many of us. Not caring to distinguish between fleeting pleasures and abiding joy, we lose ourselves in giggles and short-lived diversions that keep us amused long enough to forget we aren't blissful.

For this reluctant Ecclesiastes, the immediate challenge, self-assigned, was to see if I could find bliss in some of the places I had not yet learned to love. You have to learn to love new settings, new topographies, new environments. If you don't, then time after time you will keep returning to the same places you've been before but with different names.

I love mountains and woods and lake-shores and river fronts and seasides, love balmy islands and frigid snowscapes. To any of those I will eagerly pilgrimage. But for years I was not drawn to desert. If I had to go to desert, I passed through quickly. If I stopped, it was for a purpose.

One stop was to pay homage to unequaled American history, if *American* it should be called. After all, the Hopi Indian village of Old Oraibi in what is now northeastern Arizona has been around and continually occupied for almost a thousand years, long before there was anything called America or an Amerigo Vespucci to inspire that name. (In Florida, the venerable town of St. Augustine would like us to honor its longevity but has to do a lot of careful qualifying to claim itself as "the oldest continuously occupied, *European-established* city *and port* in the *continental* United States." It's been there shy of 500 years.)

Old Oraibi when I visited did not welcome visitors. Mostly, did not permit them. It took wangling and persistence to secure even limited admittance for our TV camerman and me – more effort than it might have needed had the good folk of Old Oraibi been Nielsen families which they happily were not. They were *off the grid* in many ways, their dusty town perched at the edge of Third Mesa, as the Indian territory designates its regions. It was desert, bleak and dry and hot but these people embodied such history and depth of cultural wealth, the chance to visit them, desert or no, was compelling.

Hunkering outside the mud and straw home of an older Hopi couple I raptly listened to stories of now and then. Of now, they spoke about why Hopi people chose to safeguard their seclusion, their privacy, to prevent their age-old ways from being diluted by the common culture outside. (Put me in mind of the Amish people of Ohio where I grew up, believing that the ways of the world around them were wrong and to avoid those ways they must largely avoid that world. We outsiders thought them strange. Outsiders tend to do that.) Some Indian peoples took the opposite tack. Next-door Navajos eagerly invited you in to buy their magnificent rugs and other crafts. Over in New Mexico, the Indians of the Taos Pueblo happily charged tourists ten dollars per person plus six dollars for each camera or cellphone brought into their village. The Hopi wanted none of that commercialism and though they knew they could not completely disengage they made their best try, so greatly did they value their traditions.

"Many, many, many years," said the Hopi gentleman whom I shall not even name, his eyes glistening with desert sun and ancestral esteem, "our people have been here. Many years. Before any people, Hopi here. This, our land, our home." His dark eyes glistened with pride in his walnut-stained face. His wife, black hair pulled back in a bun, nodded her own pride.

Things had not always been harmonious. At the dawning of the 20th century, Old Oraibi was one of the largest Hopi settlements with more than 800 people. But there were factions and dissensions that boiled over somewhere around 1906. Not in warfare or killing. The Hopi were not the sort. But in – of all things – the Indian version of tug-of-war, which they translated into a *push*-of-war. Inscribing a border line on the mesa, opposing factions took positions on either side. Those loyal to Chief You-ke-oma and his Skeleton Clan gathered on this side, those supporting chief Tawa-quap-tewa and his Bear Clan on the other and the men clustered up and began pushing. No bows and arrows or firearms, just sturdy and determined men in a scrum to shove themselves all over the line.

The Bear Clan won and almost immediately took sole possession of the village; the Skeleton Clan left and would establish the village of Hotevilla four miles away. My host and his wife took me to the spot a quarter mile from Old Oraibi where are a bear claw and a skeleton carved into the rock, marked the historic Push-of-War.

More, they gave me the great honor of descending the log pole ladder down into the village Kiva, the heart of the tribe's deliberative and spiritual life. It was mostly dark, dry and close. Dust rode the shaft of light descending the ladder. No one spoke. This was not a place for an outsider to speak nor did our Hopi friends need to. There was quiet, and in that deadening hush, that enlivening hush, that dusky hush of eternity known, echoed the beliefs that had sustained this good and worthy people for a millennium. I was awed and still feel the same as I recall the moment now.

That was one purposeful visit to desert but there was another to quite a different desert that trumped even Old Oraibi's historic longevity.

It was quite a drive to get there and most people didn't know to go. No one advertised the singular aspect of the scene; it was secreted in openness, protected by people's unknowing. It took dusty hours from L.A., across trailer park scrubland into the Mojave desert, not a seemingly auspicious site for an epiphany. Nor was the bush itself either towering or attractive. Generically, it was the most common growth in the desert and this particular specimen was low-lying, dingy, and drab. It was also astonishingly historic. They could tell from its size, the botanists who first found it in aerial photographs. Creosote plants, as they mature, spread out from a central core, spread out with new growth each year, each decade, each century, the surface center itself seeming to die away. Old creosote plants appear from the air as rings, the greater their diameters, the longer they've likely been cloning there. This particular bush, larger than any the scientists from the University of California, Riverside, till that time had seen, was seventy feet across. What did that mean? What they thought it meant, and what carbon-14 dating supported, was that the core of this dusty ring of leaves and brambles had been growing in this inhospitable place for at least *eleven thousand years*. It might be — and as far as they knew at the time it *was* — the oldest living thing on earth!

Eleven thousand years. I thought about that. That plant was already ancient when our nation was born, indeed when our continent was discovered – by white men or Hopi or anyone else. It was old when Christ was nailed to a cross in another desert a world away. It was mature when the Greeks built their Parthenon, King Solomon erected the gates of Jerusalem, little David played on his harp — those were three thousand years ago. The Druids erected Stonehenge four thousand years ago. The first Egyptian civilization built Pyramids and Sphinxes less than five thousand year ago. So to find our way to the proper point in pre-history, we must travel to before anything that could be called civilization, before metal, before money, before alphabet, before numbers — back when the Ice Age was just ending and woolly mammoths roamed the land. It was then that the seed was planted that today still grows. We looked at that plant and marveled.

We were wrong. What we were photographing, the crew and I learned to our dismay, had not, itself, been there eleven thousand years. Like most people, we were accustomed to thinking of a plant as being that formation we saw. (We're inclined to define people the same way.) But the fact is that the formation we saw was only the plant's immediate and temporary realization. The essential plant and its continuity exist in a portion not visible, beneath the surface, the root-stalk which connects this upshoot with that, serves all, and slowly but relentlessly projects the bush across desert and history.

That's how it was with the creosote bush and so, it struck me, it might be with us. What is vital and continuing and essential in us lies beneath the surface. It is something beyond our beings to which we are connected in ways that even we, its immediate and temporary realizations, may not recognize. It is, at once, the source of our connectedness, and the thrust of our continuity. Through it we share with other beings and through it we extend our own being.

It may look scruffy and nondescript, but an ancient bush out in a woebegone desert, helped teach a wanderer a powerful lesson.

If the gentle people of Old Oraibi were ennobled and ensouled by desert, if life forms of peerless antiquity thrived in desert, I needed to reassess. I read of the thirteenth century Muslim poet and theologian in Persia whose name in our language is truncated to simply Rumi, who said that trekking desert was analogous to "the spiritual quest of the Soul journeying into the infinite." Many souls have made that journey; great religions and religious figures have sprouted from that aridity. Circa 2500 B.C., the desert people of Egypt worshipped their Sun God, Ra. A millennium later, believing himself to be on personal commission, Abram, a mere human, followed the guidance across desert of the God he would teach much of the world to worship, ultimately inspiring three of the world's great religions. It was into desert that Jesus retreated for forty days and forty nights of fasting and temptation as he initiated his short-lived but undying ministry. To desert to pray went Mohammed who would be called the Prophet of Islam, that religion, too, a product of desert. And to add yet another: Where did Brigham Young – "The Moses of the Mormons," some called him – lead his Latter Day Saints but out across the mighty desert of the western United States till they reached the Great Salt Lake alongside which they would build their gold-domed religion.

The Psalmist, in desert, had been moved to pray:

> *You, God, are my God,*
> *earnestly I seek you;*
> *I thirst for you,*
> *my whole being longs for you,*
> *in a dry and parched land*
> *where there is no water.*
> *–Psalm 63*

If so much of what would be so important to the world sprang from deserts, why should anyone – why should I – spurn them? And yet ... Desert, in itself, just for fun, still held no appeal for me. Dismal, I felt it to be. I did not see beauty. I knew of many who did. Senator Barry Goldwater rhapsodized on the deserts around his Arizona home. Lord Byron longed for desert:

> *Oh that the desert were my dwelling place,*
> *With only one fair spirit for my minster.*
> *That I might forget the human race,*
> *And hating no one, love her only.*

Did I fail to share such sentiments because I was not as observant and appreciative as the Senator, as poetic as the nobleman? Or, had I not yet found just the right desert for me?

In the years-become-decades since that indelible moment, my mind has mellowed toward deserts and – as many converts can testify – there was one voice hugely responsible.

ℒ

The iconic Edward Abbey (who would have hated that descriptor) not only recorded his own lyrical love of desert but kindled the same in many others. His writings – notably his memoir, *Desert Solitaire* – tickled trekkers into trying the bleak monuments of hardened sand on sand, constructions pressed over epochs and then carved by winds into arches, ramparts and seemingly teetering towers. He wrote of these and his own life among them as he served on and off as a ranger at what became Arches National Park. Many of the tourists one finds in the town of Moab, Utah, carry in their packs or in their hearts, Abbey's paean to that corner of his beloved desert.

I read more both by and about Abbey. Down to that day when – as recounted by friends – while Abbey lay dying, still in desert although now in Arizona, he was said have enjoyed his final smile of satisfaction when assured by friends that his self-ordained burial plans would be honored. No ceremony; no cremation. His body would simply be wrapped as he wanted in one of his old sleeping bags, laid in the bed of a pickup and driven far into the remoteness of desert where friends would douse the site and themselves with ample alcohol before planting the body where, they assured him, no one would ever find him.

The more I read, the more I understood that here was my guide to learn to love new scenes, new topographies, new environments. Accordingly, to learn to love desert by and for itself. I would start with that locale the great naturalist and explorer of the West, John Wesley Powell had called *A Wilderness of Rocks* and there play a few hands of Desert Solitaire for myself.

I hit the sandy town of Moab, Utah, population 5,000, at absolutely the wrong time. Everyone was already there. They were there in such congestive numbers that the last two miles' drive into town took fully an hour and, at that, the last several blocks to my lodgings had to be made on foot. Not that cars weren't welcome in Moab that afternoon. On the contrary, *too many* cars had the town clogged for the town's annual Action Car Show and Parade. The vital arteries of Moab were thrombotic. Along what I took to be the main street, crowds stood four and five deep except where pickup trucks had been pre-positioned across sidewalks, tail gates to the street, beds filled with folding chairs accommodating patient parade gawkers. But the parade never seemed to come. Or, more accurately, *it never stopped coming.* This wasn't a normal point-to-point parade, start and stop, but something like a continuing roundabout, cars wheeling down Main Street, drivers and passengers shouting to friends and in a town that size, on a festive occasion like this, most everyone is. Then, completing the circuit, whipping back to the start to go 'round again. Louder each time. More boisterous and raucous. More fun!

Not to say more blissful. Bliss, I would only begin to experience the next morning. *Very early* the next morning. I had studied park guides and maps, also the apps that told me times and directions of sunrise and moonsets. In the guides I saw pictures of one of Arches National Park's most distinctive formations of wind-whipped stone, a natural sculpture called Balanced Rock. Albee had written about it many times

I drive beneath the overhanging Balanced Rock, 3500 tons of seamless Entrada sandstone perched on a ridiculous, inadequate pedestal of the Carmel formation, soft and rotten stone eaten away by the wind, deformed by the weight above. One of these days that rock is going to fall – in ten, fifty, or five hundred years.

Just so it isn't this morning; I have an appointment with Balanced Rock this very early morning. From the app I know by what time I need to get there while skies will be still dark, sun not yet risen but affording the muted, crepuscular light of a desert pre-dawn. Spirits move in such light. The Spirit moves in such light, and on this morning it carries me along and I follow it as much as the map as I wind up the mountain roads of the park, passing many Scenic Overlooks not yet scenic, coming around each bend, past each new silhouetted vista of rock-shadow with heightened expectation, driving and driven. I hurry, fearful that I might not get there in time, that the light might have risen too far before I get there. Maybe I'd better pull off after the next bend and shoot whatever is there. Maybe I should do that. Just one more bend. One more bend I go and ... Eureka! There it is! Balanced Rock in stunning silhouette, a deep, navy blue sky behind it, etched with a bright parenthesis moon just where the app said it would be and spangled all about with pinpoint stars.

Hurry. Car lights off. Flashers on. Grab camera and tripod. Mount camera. Lock in – what should it be? – 50 mil lens. Extend sticks. Firm them into gravel roadside. Frame shot. Set focus. Check exposure. Raise ISO. Recheck exposure. Attach shutter release cord. Perfectly still. Click shutter. Check screen replay. Raise ISO once more. Click again. Workable histogram. Click again and again, making slight variations even as nature's lighting makes its own. Work there, engrossed in craft for fifteen minutes, maybe half an hour. Considering alternative angles. Shooting, adjusting, moving, shooting, adjusting.

And through all, two things are happening within. Two minds are working. One, the technical mind, working the details of photography, translating the astonishing scene I am witnessing into something that might astonish a viewer some time hence.

The other mind at work is the mind with a tank. Call it my Bliss Tank and it has been running near empty for a long, long while, surviving on fumes. It sorely needed a refill. Now, in this scene, these calming moments, it finds bliss aplenty, waiting to be absorbed through the senses and processed by the soul.

Oh, and what's that? There, barely visible now with increased ambient light, a simple pinpoint of light noticeably brighter than the other pinpoints that were stars. This, I had not expected. Bonus! The planet Venus making a special, unheralded guest appearance in the already magical scene.

Soul-refreshing, bliss-tank-filling morning.

When I am finished, I find my wayward mind doing some whimsical math. Let's see. If Balanced Rock weighs 3500 tons, that's seven million pounds. I weigh 200. So, by weight, that rock equals 3500 me's. When will I topple?

I don't know but I know the One who knows.

Such is my first morning in Albee's lovingly remembered Desert. I am daunted however to continue my narrative. When a poet as he has already jubilated over the glories of a place like Arches, the short-call visitor is reluctant to compete even in the privacy of his own journal. Best simply to hoard the experiences, the feelings and insights of the visit, to lay them away like the desert squirrel does his treasures for winter. As for the writer's duty of informing others, urge them to read Abbey.

Off again to desert I venture, determined to continue my education, discern the beauty that others saw, and learn the dignity and passion camouflaged by persistent bleakness. The word "arid" sometimes means "Lacking in moisture; dry." But it can also mean "Lacking in interest, excitement or meaning." I could not change the former but I could work on the latter.

On my next expedition, however, my choice of companions, a dozen camera chums, challenges my mission. Oh, we will have wonderful photographic times, to be sure. However,

I knew not what to expect when I came
To the desert with friends from across the land
Believers and non-, theists and a-
Out each morning to waken the day
Calling its colors to splash 'cross the sand,
The sun to patiently reclaim

Its rightful role – but not quite yet
Let light linger warm and shadows long
As photographs and memories
Are caught and fixed. Then, taking ease,
Each can lift up each's song
Of praise or denial, doubt or debt

Actually, there is no doubt
No doubt expressed as we share the morn

Believers don't doubt to whom debt is owed,
Who, upon us these gifts has bestowed;
Who created the scenes that adorn
Our lives, ourselves, within, without.

Unbelievers don't doubt; they trust in the known,
Facts on electronic library shelves
(How impoverished, circumscribed by the act
Of trusting only provable fact.)
Worshipping knowledge, they worship themselves
They, their own idols, they alone
For myself I can't conceive
Of being left without the glow
Of understanding that all I am seeing
Is testimony to His being
Let others believe in what they know
In the desert, I know what I believe

There is bliss in knowing of one's believing here in the parched panorama. Parched, and yet, and yet. . .

. . . as though to make all right,
Flare dizzily, dazzling desert blooms
Growing here, so one assumes,
To be the melodies of grace
In otherwise a tuneless place
Space of sallow, subtle hues.
Did nature here not get the news
That bright and splashy are the way
The world prefers its palette today?

Forget today; think of a time
Millennia past in a distant land;
No cactus there but abundant sand

And men the world thought of as lowly
But in whom it was that grew a holy
Faith to supplant the culture of many
Gods where men could worship any
God they thought to be most giving
With a culture of only a single living
God – El, or Elohim –
Many ways to speak of him
Once, as desert years went by,
People called their God El Shaddai
Or an unpronounceable tetragram
Till finally, God told them "I am – I AM"

This happened in desert such as I slandered
Before as a bleak and tuneless land
But tunes that arose there those ancient days
Are now the historic hymns of praise
We sing remembering Abraham
And the blissful desert that gave us all
The Great I AM

The great **I AM.** How I would need him with me when I made my hardest desert trip of all, I and some friends new and old.

It was a haunting journey with three entertainment celebrities to the parched, starvation lands of sub-Saharan Africa, desert desolate and deathly. A pleasure trip, this was not, taken for the purpose of bringing three Hollywood stars – comic actor of TV and film, Dick Van Patten, Broadway child star then film actress Patty (Anna) Duke, and the recent "Roots" miniseries star young LeVar Burton together with the myriad of unknown faces suffering unconscionable human privation. Bring a TV crew along to show and tell the rest of the world in hope of raising sympathy and money for relief assistance.

I documented parts of the trip in *Finding Moosewood, Finding God*. I told how upon arrival at a place we had never heard of, Nouakchott, capital of the West African nation of Mauritania, Father Bud, his Hollywood guests and we TV folk were rushed off to visit the first of what would be many wrenchingly similar sites, an emergency feeding station run by the Catholic Relief Services where the impoverished and displaced could find life-saving sustenance for themselves and their babies. For many of us this was a first exposure to the bloated bellies that did not come from overeating, but were the ironic mocking of severe malnutrition, near-starvation. Profound sadness glazed the eyes of mothers holding babies they could not feed because they themselves had not enough nutrition to make mother's milk. Flies crawled on babies' faces, not one of them with strength to shoo the pests away. The germs they carried would soon infect, or already had.

Seeing these mothers, these babies, which of us, the fortunate, the very, very fortunate, would not be numbed and humbled? Anna with no hesitation began kissing and embracing, instinctively doing "unto the least of these." LeVar was also instantly hands-on. Only Dick balked for a moment, clearly, at first, overwhelmed by it all, of what he had and they had not.

For many days that would be the awful disconnect between realities. Between our lives and the lives of the people we met, there seemed an unbridgeable chasm. We would witness the pitiable state of their lives, and would pity, then head back our hotels and full-course dinners. How could we do that? How could we eat knowing they could not? How could we sleep in comfort when they had none? I asked the priest leading our mission on behalf of Catholic Relief Services. Father Bud Keisser could be a great, joking, fun-loving companion. He could also be a wise and reverent man of God. "Jack, we do what we can with what we are given. And what we are given most abundantly, our little group, are compassion and caring, yes, but also the means to reach millions and millions of people who may also be found to be compassionate. Those people will be drawn to LeVar and Anna and Dick. They will listen to them and pay attention to what they are experiencing here. And you and your crew will make that possible. That is what we can do and it is not insignificant. Don't underestimate the gifts we are given or can give. "

From Mauritania, we traveled to Senegal, then to Djibouti, again a place many of our group had not heard of before, sticking out like a gangrenous thumb atop the horn of Africa, a desolate place. Which is to say, one *more* desolate place. In many ways these days were harder on Dick than the rest of us. He was not a worldly man. Had traveled little; feared flying. The horror he found at each new stop was not only beyond his experience, but beyond his comprehension.

There was a strange moment one morning as we were being driven several hours across the desert to a remote relief center. Our drivers had amply stocked our vehicles with cases of bottled water against the heat and dryness of the day. I rode with Dick. When we were well clear of anything we would interpret as civilization, only sand, flat and hot on all sides, we spotted in the distance a small cluster of people. Dick marveled "What do you imagine they're doing way out here?"

I said simply, "They live here."

"Live where?"

"Here."

"In the desert?"

"They're Bedouin, nomadic people of the desert."

He couldn't fathom that. "Amazing," he said and it was clear from his facile face that he was amazed.

A bit farther along, we saw another group of people, these closer to the road and Dick was thinking. "It must be so hard for them out here. So dry, so hot. They must really be thirsty." He told the driver to stop when we got to the people, whereupon Dick got out, went around to the back of our SUV and grabbed one of the cases of water we had stockpiled for the expedition and headed over to the little knot of people talking as he went. He spoke a language the people couldn't understand, of course, anymore than he could decipher theirs as the woman at the core of the group spoke volubly at him. Back and forth it went each person importuning the other to no avail.

In the front seat of our vehicle, our driver laughed softly. He was the only one of us who appreciated what was happening out there as our friend, moved by what he thought to be the unfortunate plight of the Bedouin suffering from terrible thirst tried to give them his case of water and couldn't understand why they wouldn't accept.

While, at the same time, the Bedouin stood there with tall earthenware urns around them trying to sell this no doubt weary and thirsty traveler some of their water. That was their business. Profound cross-cultural misunderstanding.

Farther along, we came to a clutch of simple huts, a small, dusky village and, through our driver/interpreter got ourselves in to talk with one of the mothers about her family's lives. There was the mother and father who was outside the hut and they had a ten-year old girl who was off fetching water from the nearest spring a mile or so distant. When, at length, I saw her approaching, the bright-faced child serving as one more beast of burden, I asked the driver to inquire what the child, her chores completed, would likely do for play. I was thinking some sort of game with rocks or sticks; maybe she had a ball of some sort. Maybe a chase game with other kids. He asked. He listened.

"Nothing," he translated to me. "She says girl does no play. Never play."

"Never?"

He asked.

"Never. She says never play."

That stunned me. A child who in ten years of living had never played! This was not a nice world. And that was not to be my final notice.

She was a passing acquaintance, nothing more, and I knew that the moment we met.

Her name was Djamila. I say "was" because … let me tell.

We reached the ultimate destination of our day's drive across the Ali Sabieh district of Djibouti to find a rude hospital where scarcely-trained doctors and nurses tried, with severely limited means, to provide at least palliative if not curative care for some of the worst victims of starvation we would see anywhere along our trip. This was where I met the girl I want to tell you about. Want to tell you because the vision of her still – these many years later – I find ineradicable.

Escorted into a hospital room, I found a nurse in soiled scrubs examining a girl on a soiled cot. The girl was sickly slender, expressionless yet somehow serenely beautiful; without speaking, she stunned. The chart on the foot of her bed read: "Djamila Osman." I presumed as years passed I might no longer remember that name but never until never would I forget those eyes. Dark and fathomless, as though she were one of those poignant big-eyed drawings by the American artist of the sixties, Margaret Kean, the exaggeratedly large eyes looking up at you, entreating beyond language and ken. They wounded.

I figured the girl to be four or five though the nurse said she was probably twice that but diminished physically and dispirited emotionally by the life she had been forced to live. Forced, please understand, not by nature, not by desert itself, but by the implacable cruelty and greed of uncaring men. Throughout these writings, I try to be be gender-neutral, but I cannot be here. The cruelty and greed were solely the acts of uncaring *men!* Men, as usual, were the Warmakers, men, the Destroyers. Beauty, destroyed by Ugly. It is not unfair to say that my personal umbrage toward deserts springs partly from what too often just such men have done to just such girls – and their families and kinsmen and millions more. To such unspeakable predators, all are prey.

The nurse knew the story, had gotten it from Djamila's father. His wife, Djamila's mother had been raped to death by men who rampaged through their village one day. Escaping the men Warmakers, men food-thieves and men crop confiscators, her father took Djamila and two sisters, carrying what they could on their backs and walking out across the sands to a place far distant where, perhaps, word was, maybe, they might find relief. They had not much food to bring with them on the trek but brought all they could. How to dole it out at the end of day? The traditional order of precedence in such matters was one of primogeniture. Djamila was the oldest child. When food started running short, she and her father got meager rations, the younger children none. Those lost strength as wobbly weeks wore on and one by one fell to the desert floor not to rise again.

Only she and her father remained as on they plodded. It was only after Djamila herself was so weakened by malnutrition and she, the last of the children, could not continue that her father began carrying her frail frame as finally in the distance they could see the refugee camp and meager hospital where now I found her. I did not find him. His last, selfless exertion meant to save her had exhausted his final reserves. He died at the hospital threshold. Djamila was the only survivor of the Osman family, and the nurse told me that she too, that beautiful, haunting and haunted child, doubtless, would not last long. Damn the desert and the savagery bred within it!

I stayed with her most of an hour, talking though knowing she did not understand except that perhaps she could understand the tone of my prayers for her. Maybe. Then, I was told by our driver that we were going to have to leave. I looked at her one last time, her large eyes burning holes in my heart. Not that they meant to do. I think if they were attempting to convey anything their message was elemental: *Why?* And maybe, *Kind Face, can you not help?*

No, dear child, I cannot. I could do nothing but stare into those deep, dark eyes and hurt for her hurting. And pray. It was prayer, though, that would not, could not assuage in me the guilt of inadequacy. "Don't underestimate the gifts we are given or can give," Father Bud had told me a few days before. But *Damn!* For Djamila, dear dying Djamila, I had no gifts to give.

She was a passing acquaintance, nothing more. I knew that the moment we met.

WAS IT A MURRE?

Meeting death is not easy. Confronting death that's inevitable rips you apart. Even harder, though, is to suddenly, unexpectedly stumble upon death, countless and unexplained Mary Jo and I are out for a chilled morning walk in what seems a paradise. *Seems.* Even at first, it's not what we expected but then when exploring the unexpected can be the most exciting travel of all.

So stepping onto this Oregon beach on a brisk-whipping day, we walk along, scuffing sand, turning jacket collar up against the late summer cold, sun high, sky azure, wind tugging half-hearted clouds into sweet strings of taffy. Idyllic day, so at first it appears.

The beach runs for miles, broad and unpeopled. To our left as we walk south, weathered-wood houses with shuttered windows stand at parade rest, eyes to the ocean unseeing. It's Wednesday, weekenders gone. Sands have forgotten their footsteps. The beach rests.

Except a beach never rests. Of all things, all places in nature, more than any, a beach is restless. As unceasing as the waves that created it are the waves that each day re-create it. Sun flashes on the flanks of those waves as they frolic in their playful work.

This is a special stretch of beach. Tides, flowing then ebbing with muscular determination deposit such generosities of driftwood that a local tourist brochure claims that this is "The Greatest Stand of Driftwood" in the nation.

Except it doesn't stand. It lies, lolls, sprawls, squats, hunkers, kneels, poses and postures, dances, does a *plié, piqué* and *grand jeté*. It is an astonishing aggregation of logs and limbs, of stumps, branches, chunks, hunks and burls – a fantasy menagerie of derelict creatures, some quite exhausted from their long swim, fetched up on this beach to rest and be admired: here a turtle-burl, there a branch-dragon, now a limb-shark, then a voodoo stump. What happy hunting for those curious craftsmen whose delight is implanting clockworks into carved creatures' abdomens.

All right. Here are drift and waves and sand and sun, an idyllic beach, broad and endless and abandoned save for us – and something is wrong.

Terribly wrong.

Abandoned save for us. That's the problem. Of apparent life on this restless beach, as far as we can see there are we two people and nothing more.

No birds! But always on a beach there are birds, hopping, dipping, diving, feeding – sandpipers, terns, plovers, dunlins, gulls, willets, turnstones, stilts, maybe skimmers, even pelicans – always. But not today, not here.

Why?

The answer starts to appear a hundred yards along, in the sand beside a craggy crotch of driftwood where we discover the carcass of a bird, a good-sized bird with black head and back, soft white down on the belly and undertail. A murre, I believe; I am not sure.

Unusual to find a bird's body on a beach. And – wait – not just one. No, over there, in a sand hollow a dozen feet away lies another. Same kind of bird. Same sort of death?

Thoughts dart to other beaches walked, warm or cold, this land or others. Always, to be sure, they were strewn with death's deposits, from tiny coquina shells sprinkling pastel across the sugar sands of Sanibel in Florida, to bleached whale skeletons in Alaska. Death is not uncommon to beaches. Sand itself is its product. But death of birds is usually not advertised. So how it is that here on an Oregon beach there are one and then two dead birds and now there lies a third and beyond it one more? And as slowly, reluctantly, eyes attune to the silent scene they see several, then many, then scores, maybe even hundreds of feathered carcasses along this morbid stretch. A hideous panorama in black and white – with gashes of color.

Look closely. On the underside of a carcass, see a puff of clean, white down rudely ripped by a streak of red-brown, a belly torn open by an uncaring predator (while victim still barely lived?), entrails devoured.

The mind screams:

> God, dear God, why in Your Own Name did you make us animals so terribly cruel? Why couldn't we all be herbivorous, live in harmony and, for population control, restrain birth rates? Why not? Sorry, God. Just questions. In matters like this, as You know, questioning is all we humans can do.

Beaches incite unanswerable questions. Each person, on a beach, becomes a less articulate Anne Morrow Lindbergh. That is the lure. More than the softening warmth of sun, or the pressing tickle of sand-between-toes, or the rhythm of waves, the therapy of a walk on a beach is reflection. The beach teases us with prospects of not having to think but then, when we get here, gets us thinking more than ever. And if we cannot answer the questions it incites, the fact we cannot is important to re-learn.

Birds on a beach. Dead by the hundreds. Why?

Walk on. The mind tries to hide, the eyes not to see. Use other senses. Let skin feel the slap of crisp air; let taste buds savor its salt; let ears attune to the pulse of the surf; and nostrils take in the pungency of wet wood and kelp. Walk on keen to only those senses for a mile or so until, finally, on a beach still littered with what the eyes do not want to see, there is a sight so compelling they cannot ignore. The sight is a single bird, black and white as the others, its body deposited on the sand like the rest but this bird, unlike those, still lives. Barely.

For this moment. It lies huddled as though nested here in the sand. First seen, it might appear a placid picture of nature's repose. But it does not fly as we approach. It cannot. Whatever killed the others seems to be killing this one. Slowly.

We watch her. (Why do we assume it a female? Because it is pitiable and females seem more worthy of our caring?) We watch as she probes about with her beak. Tentatively but vainly she pecks at a twig, picks it up, tests it, then drops it. It is the only object within reach but it is of no use. It is not food nor water – nor life. She will die. She looks up at us. She looks away.

We are stupid. A creature lies dying before us and we do nothing. We know nothing to do. The bird will die as others have died and confronted by that inevitability, we, the most potent of earth's creatures, are impotent.

Tomorrow in a book store a man will tell us he read in the local paper about some micro-organism that has infected parts of the avian population. That knowledge might lead to research that might help the avian population. In the future.

But today, I am not talking about "avian population." I'm mourning beautiful black and white birds that have died, or are dying, each by itself, no one caring.

No one caring. That is one small advantage humans have. When we are dying, if we're lucky, someone cares. And knows our name.

Are they murres? Was she a murre? Do I know her name?

We turn away as people do confronting death. More briskly now we head back up the beach whence we came, passing death while trying to talk about styles of shoreside houses, taffiness of clouds and who would want a lump of driftwood with a clock in its belly anyhow.

Humans are the only creatures on earth who contemplate death, the only animals that know they are going to die. Faced with that awareness, what do they do? They try to forget. Some days, like today, they cannot.

We walk on in silence, a silence unanswered.

MOUNTAINS, MUIR AND A CUP OF TEA

W hen I find myself bewildered by dilemmas in nature, I seek out a man wise about nature. When flummoxed by a puzzle permitted by God, I turn to a man of God. Sometimes, they are the same man.

Thinking of John Muir two lines come to mind. They are lines I happily hoard. Not until putting together these thoughts, however, did I learn that one of those lines is not Muir at all. It sounds like him; I always thought it was. The other line which is Muir without doubt, I regularly turn to to re-kindle my own adoration.

Start with the first:

Bring me men to match my mountains . . . That, I thought, was Muir, the great Scottish-American nature adorer, imagining the voice of his beloved California speaking that plea. And, indeed, his call was answered, many stalwart mountain-matching men pouring into the Golden State year after year.

I started playing with the line when we moved to Florida, a state whose highest mountain may be at Walt Disney World and whose greatest ascents by which most Floridians are challenged are the speed bumps at their local Publix. Accordingly, my febrile imagination projected my newly-adopted Florida voicing the identical call I ascribed to Muir – *Bring me men to match my mountains* – and getting its wish. In poured the flaccid and weary, pale and frail, retirees who too often would find their lives foreshortened because they had retired *from* something, not *to* something. Such were Florida's mountain-matchers.

Do I fit that category? I answer by changing the subject. After all, this has nothing to do with John Muir. It wasn't his line anyhow. It was, in fact, from someone named Sam Walter Foss, a small town librarian in Massachusetts in the 1890's who wrote a short poem every day for local newspapers and one of them read:

> *Bring me men to match my mountains*
> *Bring me men to match my plains*
> *Men with empires in their purpose*
> *And new eras in their brains*

The first line of that quatrain gained such renown it was inscribed on a granite walkway called the Warrior Ramp at the US Air Force Academy hard by the towering mountains of Colorado until it was removed in 2003 to acknowledge the female cadets who also "matched" those mountains.

He grew up in Scotland, John Muir, a child with a stern Calvinist father who demanded of the son rote recitation of Bible verses and whipped him for mistakes. Only at home with his loving mother or outdoors amid the swells and swales of the lush green countryside, gazing out at the raging waters of the North sea from the Dunbar, Scotland waterfront would young John find relief from the beatings. Nature was peace, surcease.

His father moved the family to the United States, to the midwest, where young John marveled at "the wilderness all about", wilderness that would become his life. Despite (or because of?) a terrible accident he suffered while working in a machine shop, jamming the point of a file into an eye which immediately went blind, followed a while later by sympathetic blindness in his other eye. His dearest friend philosophized: perhaps God had chosen to give Muir "the eye within the eye, to see in all natural objects the realized ideas of His mind." Even as he recovered sight in the uninjured eye and and could start to make out silhouettes in the other, his best friend told him she was sure this accident would lead him to his place in life

It was a long trip, a thousand mile foot-wander across the country, down south, out west, taking in the astonishing variety of life and scenery, birds and animals, bayous and plains, mountains and flower-speckled meadows, and through all, seeing nature with his inner sight as well as his compromised outer vision. It thrilled and inspired him. No place moreso than the grand valley of Yosemite. That, he knew instantly, would be his heart's home. He would continue to travel in many directions but always, gratefully, return "home."

As Muir matured he found his life being guided, he wrote, by two books – the Book of God and the Book of Nature. The first, the Bible he had been forced to study and the second, the entire compendium of creation he found all around him, having come "straight from the hand of God, uncorrupted by civilization and domestication."

Both of those books he came to know better than most of us ever will. His harshly administered servitude memorizing Bible passages, rather than souring him on belief had made him more keenly appreciative. As an adult, he could recite virtually all of the New Testament and much of the Old. And not just recite but understand and live by He knew what Paul meant in Romans 1:20

> *From the time the world was created, people have seen the earth and sky and all that God made. They can clearly see his invisible qualities—his eternal power and divine nature. So they have no excuse whatsoever for not knowing God.*

John Muir knew God and for the rest of his life did His work, becoming the preeminent advocate for the appreciation and preservation of nature in his adopted homeland. It was through his insistence and his persistence that congress made his beloved Yosemite a National Park, and designated Sequoia National Park as well. Today his name is honored and his memory secured by the National Monument named for him in northern California, Muir Woods, a mystical place of redwoods as towering as an immigrant's dreams.

He was a great scientist and a great believer. It surprises some folks to think that those two need not be mutually exclusive, that a person of science can be also a person of faith. But John Muir was, and many today are.

My disagreement with Muir is only in the mountains he chose as the grandest in the land. He was a man of the west; they were western mountains he would celebrate and aggrandize. My preference, contrarily, is for the mountains he left behind.

Is it because I am no longer young that I tend to depreciate youth and honor age? Is that why, when thinking of mountains, my mind is drawn not to his sharp, high peaks of the west. I have enjoyed those. Have backpacked and photographed, skied and hiked among them for many years; camped in the shadow of towering Sierra peaks; ridden snowcats across Yosemite high meadows feet-deep in snow; snowmobiled wintry Yellowstone; traveled The Road To The Sun slanting across the Continental Divide at Glacier National Park; scheduled a visit to Montana's Lake MacDonald for that precise time in the fall that dozens, even hundreds, of American Bald Eagles come down from their mountain aeries to feed on spawning salmon in an unsurpassed spectacle of our insignia bird; tossed my thoughts into the deep of Canada's Lake Louise; and found their echoes rising from lonely Lac Beauvert. That lake is in the heart of Canada's Jasper National Park and home to an innumerable array of species whose friendship in those days delighted me.

So, yes, I love the young mountains of the West but beyond those, I love and respect the older, rolling mounts of the east. Mountains they surely are, those Appalachians (once called Alleghenies) – those Cumberlands and Great Smokies and Blue Ridge, or farther north Poconos, Catskills, Berkshires, and farther yet, the Presidential

Range, the White mountains, on up to Katahdin in Maine. In all these, but especially the lower stretch of Appalachia I revel not just for what they are today but for what they used to be. I said I honor age. There are geologic formations in these lower Appalachians that date back some *eleven hundred million years* In their time they were likely the tallest mountains anywhere, taller than the Rockies or the Alps. They are surely older than those. The mountains of southern Appalachia are quite likely the oldest mountains in the world! What an honor it is to visit them. What a privilege to dwell among them.

Escaping Atlanta, drive north on 575 which becomes highway 515. On either side, and especially up ahead roll vistas that deceive. They appear to be hills on their way to becoming mountains. They roll and softly tumble, tumble and recede in distance and tone. What seem up close to be vivid green mountains become muted green hills at mid-distance, fading at last to monochrome prominences on a colorless horizon.

They appear, curiously, to be growing in stature and importance as their vista recedes. And that is the lie. These are not hills becoming mountains. They have already been mountains.

Driving up #515 in north Georgia, follow what structural geologists identify as the Murphy Syncline. In their language, a syncline is where the earth has been folded and the bottom of each fold is designated as a *syncline.* (The top, an *anticline.*) Think of it as a great trough in the landscape that extends, in this case, all the way up to the little town of Blue Ridge fifty or sixty miles north. On either side along the run are hills that drivers of cars and trucks will mostly disregard but that thrill geologists with their astonishing catalog of rock strata recounting most every period, era and epoch in known history. Crystalline formations, rocks igneous, metamorphic and sedimentary – anything historians of the earth know, odds are they can find here in the lower Appalachians – these Blue Ridge formations and the upcoming Smokies. Proud vestiges of the world's oldest mountains!

And of much greater importance to me is the fact noted by one of Appalachia's proudest chroniclers, Georgia's former governor and

U.S. Senator, Zell Miller: To him, these mountains are where "The world's largest, most varied, and probably first deciduous forest (was) spawned, nurtured, preserved and showcased." He thought them to be the world's most "perfected" mountains. Not just picturesque but "perfected."

With a home in their midst and awed by that perfection, I do not dissent. From the deck of our place in the Blue Ridge foothills, poised some fifteen feet above the forest floor as it slopes down toward the ever-glistening waters of Mountaintown Creek, I am cosseted in that variety of which Miller wrote. There are conifers, to be sure – the dark blue-green fans of spreading hemlock; the proliferating pines with their new spring growth like lighted candles atop darker green candelabra. There are spruce and fir, keeping green year round, but this is principally a forest of broad-leafed trees. Deciduous, from the Latin, *decidere*, meaning "to fall off" as their leaves do each autumn. And there we have a problem.

We love fall colors; every one does. (Save, perhaps, those impressed into inevitable raking duties). But autumn leaves, musical as the phrase has come to seem, mislead us. Too easy it is to think of the flaming leaves of the red maple, afire in the fall, or the burnished copper of beech or the yellows and oranges of oak, birch and poplar, as being but the costumes those trees don for their final hours – their vibrant shrouds. We think this way because we have assumed through the year that we have been looking at trees as they really are, adorned with leafy verdure. If we but knew or reminded ourselves that the greens deciduous trees sport are only their working clothes. Trees, in season, are hard at their jobs. Their work on one hand is most honorable; they busy themselves producing and storing the nutrition they will need over a coming winter with its predictable privations of cold and abundant sunlight. Trees, that is, are looking to the future and working with diligence to be ready for it. Which is to say that with no brains with which to think, trees "outthink" some humans. With no capacity to plan, they plan. In the sunlit warmth of summer, they "know" to be busy using chlorophyll to produce the sustenance that will nourish them through the summer and then, stored away, keep them going through the winter.

Our politicized society lately has come to rail against the carbon dioxide (CO_2) created by exhaling humans, flatulent cows and working factories all of which, it is argued, cause global climate change. That is arguable and is argued but this is not: CO_2 gives life to plants and thus, indirectly, to us. In the process of photosynthesis, plants using molecules of chlorophyll, photoreceptors capable of capturing energy from light, transform CO_2 and water into carbohydrates like glucose which are the basic foodstuff of trees and bushes. And since humans derive nutrition either directly or indirectly from plants, that means that chlorophyll and photosynthesis create our sustenance too. Additionally, the process expels a byproduct which plants don't need but we do: oxygen. It is a complex cycle of continuing balance, interdependence and renewal. Many think this just happened, unguided. I don't have enough faith to believe that.

There is one more important result of the process of photosynthesis. As long as it is working, chlorophyll absorbs the light across most of the color spectrum, notably excepting that part of the spectrum between 500-600 nanometers. In that range, very little of the light is absorbed; most is reflected. Since that is the green segment of the spectrum, summer leaves appear green. Only after chlorophyll starts breaking down in the chill of early autumn do leaves lose that green and their underlying hues start to emerge. Which means leaves are like people. Only after they stop working to make the green do they show themselves for what they really are.

When living in woods, one ought to know woods. Not just, *oh, there are a lot of trees here.* That's the way you might think in a city. *Oh, there are a lot of people here.* In a city you may have no interest in knowing any more about them. They are people you do not know and never will or need to; why bother? Such may be the attitude in cities; you know so many people already; your dance card is full.

However, when you live distant from other people, remote, not totally secluded, but less often entangled with groups, let alone crowds, let alone hordes, then you have a reasonable chance to tighten your focus. Yes, there are a lot of trees around in the welcoming woods and your assignment, gregarious friend of the woods, is to get to know them better.

And here, I finally get to my second quotation from John Muir. The one that really was. In his book The American Forests he wrote:

> *The forests of America, however slighted by man, must have been a great delight to God; for they were the best he ever planted.*

I survey my friends.

Tallest, most impressive in the neighborhood are the arrow-straight trunks of the oaks, trees that can grow a hundred feet high and the specimens around our cabin are pushing that. Study as I may, from Boy scout days to now, I still can't reliably tell them apart. Pin oaks, I know, and bur and white; I have trouble with red and scarlet and black.

Also, in what Zell Miller deemed "The world's largest, most varied, and probably first deciduous forest" here in Appalachia we meet and get to know maples, mostly red maples, the spectacular bonfires of autumn, their flaming colors thrilling us not with premonitions of death but celebrations of abundant and flourishing life, the life those leaves synthesized and stored before their well-earned winter hiatus.

There are abundant tuliptrees, sometimes called tulip poplar though they are not technically poplars, closer to magnolias, each leaf shaped in maturity to suggest the profile of a tulip flower. As a kid in Ohio they were among the first trees I learned to identify, so distinct the leaf. What I did not know then was that this species, spread across the eastern U.S., is, here in the southeast, the tallest hardwood and one of the most valuable, a fast growing tree reaching as high as 185 feet, and being shade intolerant it will often be found rising the first hundred or more feet before its branches and leaves begin, affording the harvester with long, clear timber. The tulip trees around us are shorter, not needing the height to get their due ration of sunlight. But each one reminds us of nature's seemingly endless ways of adjusting to situations, which is to say, of God's power of endless adaptation in His continuing Creation.

The tuliptree is a major honey source and if the honey made from it is too dark for some people's table taste, it is appreciated by bakers.

Bees also produce an admirable honey from what would seem the wrongly named Sourwood tree, while from the nearby Sweetgum tree, *nothing!* At least no honey though the tree does get its name from the perceived sweetness of its gum, compared to amberbris. The sweetgum is a tall hardwood, widespread and valuable, it's hard wood used in everything from railroad ties to cigar boxes. That's versatility. The most striking things about the sweetgum tree, though, are things you should hope don't strike you. The fruit is a hard little spiked ball remindful of a miniature version of a medieval flail swung on an iron chain. It's a cross between a brown golf ball and a porcupine. Falling from the tree onto an unhatted head gets your sharp attention.

Since my Scout days I have known the Sassafras tree's distinctive mitten-shaped leaves (sometimes with just one thumb, sometimes with two) and it's potential for being brewed into a respectable campfire tea. We have a few of those around our place now as well and they are welcome reminders of a fitting way to start a verdant summer day.

Cup in hand, reliving the refreshing flavor of sassafras tea, I'm inclined to sit here all morning, here on the deck of our mountainside "tree house." What am I doing here? Gazing at greens. Looking up at trees, looking down at trees, looking out at trees while nestled among trees, I am part of the woods, imbibing the luxuriance of sourwood and sweet gum, hemlock and sycamore, poplar and pine. Drinking in, too, the cool moistness that enhances the gloss and the depth of their colors.

Their colors – this time of year – green. All fundamentally the same color, yet all different – just a bit different, somewhat different, almost totally different, different. Never have I encountered such a profusion of greens in one array. I confront a broad canvas intriguingly painted with limited palette. A hi-def, widescreen panorama showing nothing on its display but multifold variations of green. Some have more yellow, some, more blue. Some are lightly saturated, some superbold. Some are bright of luminance, some quite dim. But all are green.

My wife, an artist, has quite a collection of art supply websites she uses. I check one, searching to see how many green paints I find. These are *some*:

Grass green, Phthalo green, Cadmium green, Sap green, Winsor green, Lime green, Shadow green, Jenkin's green, Cinnabar green, Old Holland bright green, Antique green, Water green, Acid Green Fluorescent, and Leaf green (which looks like none of the leaves in the panoply before me). There are Permanent green, Pearl Interference green, Shiva green, Kelly green, Olive green, Hooker's green, Ash green, Turquoise green, Brilliant Yellow green, Green Earth, Cobalt Green Hue, Permanent Green Deep, Old Holland Golden green, Metallic green, Shadow green, Winsor Green Blue Shade, Green Grey Light, Green Gray Dark, Blockx green, Bottle green, Aqua green, Marine green, Viridian green, Chromium Oxide green, Emerald green, Prussian green, Interference green, Lawn green, green Umber, Bohemian green Earth, Absinthe green, Celadon green, Meadow green, Jungle green, Barium green, Lascaux green, Brilliant green, Cupric green, Compose green, Ice green, Monestial green, Perylene green, Japanesque green gold, Oriental green, Green Apple, Luminous green, Phthalocyanine green, Bamboo green, Tropical green, Baryte green, Shock green, Sap Green Lake Extra, Veronese green, Deep green, Courbet green, and that list – exhausting if not exhaustive – takes me only a quarter of the way through the listings of greens from this one art supply house's website. How many more can there be? How many greens are there?

To start: what do we mean by green? To color scientists, successors of Aristotle, Goethe and Newton, the color green refers to light in the spectral wavelength between 490nm and 560nm. Green occupies the widest wedge of any color in the spectral wheel. That is, there are more variations of green than of any other color.

I think I see them all this morning.

How? How do I see them? That's the other half of the scientific equation. First, the wavelength of light emitted or reflected by an object and then how that wavelength is received by human eye and brain. Here the color scientist leads us into the discussion of cones, the color receptors of the retina. Basically, humans are said to be trichromatic, with three types of color receptors or cones. One perceives blues and blue-violets. One, greens and the other, reds.

(In the same way, the digital sensors in most of today's cameras break light down by what is called a Bayer Array to activate the appropriate receptors among the sensor's photosites, instructing each to respond with the appropriate intensity to create the colors intended in that area of pixels. Red, green and blue. RGB.)

Some people are shown to be tetrachromatic, with four pigments instead of three in the cone cells of their retinas. Probably half of all women have this enhanced ability to distinguish colors.

I don't have it but still am overwhelmed by all the greens I can distinguish this morning.

The color scientists who filled us with the previous palaver about *Cones, Bayer Array,* and *Tetrachromaticity* and who assure us that there doubtless are more greens than any other color at that point begin to fudge. As a photographer, I know that when working up a color image I'm dealing with three aspects to consider: HSL – Hue (the basic color), Saturation (the intensity of said color) and Luminance (its brightness). All can be adjusted a myriads of ways resulting, each adjustment, in a different "color." Who can blame the fudgers' ambivalence when they posit simply that there have to be "millions" of greens?

And, as I said, I think I see them all this morning. At least all that my limited, trichromatic retinas can give me. Which is to say all that God wants me to behold which is bounty aplenty for me.

The drooping boughs of the eastern hemlock are mostly clad in a dark green tinged with blue, the colors muted in these crepuscular hours. At the end of each bough, each branchlet, though is a lighter, brighter tip, and that is a welcome signal of success. The species has been falling victim in recent years to a destructive wave of aphids that are killing forests of hemlock. Guided by our local Ag authorities, we took prophylactic action last year, creating holes in the ground every foot or so around the circumference at the base of each trunk, and pouring into each hole with a turkey baster the prescribed mixture of chemicals to protect the tree from the invaders. Now, a year later, how glad we are to find the bright tips on the boughs marking healthy spurts of new growth, marking life, salvation, resurrection.

The greens of the poplar are different. Where the hemlock boughs are predominantly dim and bluish, the poplar leaves, especially now as light grows, appear more luminous and tinged with yellow. The trunk of the poplar nearest is clothed in other green, green hosiery from ground up to first-branch, a vine of some sort volunteering to complete the poplar's verdant ensemble.

There are greens I see even on what at first seem bare branches, the greens of lichen and moss.

As streaming sun amps, every green in the palette brightens. And now, unexpectedly into the verdure flies an arresting counterpoint. Onto an empty limb of a sourwood tree alights a cardinal, a brilliant red male cardinal, well aware, I like to think, of the stunning accent he creates for the tableau. There are only a few other spots of non-green in the scene. The pale yellow-brown of one dead leaf on a vine, a wrinkled brown leaf from last year's fall stuck in a hemlock bough. All else in the scene is one of those millions of tones of green except, now on a branch otherwise bare, the cardinal! *Oh, yes, bird, we see you. We certainly see you.*

My wife once did an exercise, a painting of a male cardinal that would not be initially obvious. How could she do that, depict such a boldly conspicuous creature without its being conspicuous? She met the challenge by filling her canvas, first, with flowers from our Florida garden, a couple of plants she had brought home from church years before and planted only to watch them multiply until in season we had a six foot high wall of poinsettias. Those flowers she laid in acrylics onto her canvas, one after another until the canvas was almost filled. Into the one opening remaining, then, she painted the bird, Same colors, same tones, the black streaks of feather echoing the shadows between blossoms. The bird "lost" among the flowers. The conspicuous cardinal rendered inconspicuous. And, I imagine, cardinally unhappy.

How much more satisfying for his colleague on our sourwood branch this morning to have the whole green scene to himself! Some birds enjoy standing out. (Mostly, males. No comment.)

I cannot talk about green without thinking of a friend, a dear hyphenated friend, John Seerey-Lester. In the art world, John is virtually without peer, one of the most honored, esteemed, even knighted wildlife artists. A Brit, recently and proudly become American citizen, John, in his artworks, be they oils, acrylics or watercolored pencil sketches, takes great, evasive lengths to avoid the color green, especially a bright, vivid green like spring grass. He'd rather wait and depict browned out grasses. You will rarely find green on his palette. If he needs a green for a special purpose he'll mix it, blending, perhaps, cad yellow, ultramarine, maybe raw umber and a bit of Payne's gray. Why his seemingly inapt aversion? Because, he says, he just doesn't like bright green.

I have felt that way. Not this day to be sure, but once – and I remember it well. I had traveled with cameras and friends to an American rainforest. The prospect thrilled, the luxuriance of the foliage softened and muted by characteristic mists and rains and fog. Great pictures possible.

But it didn't happen that way. The week we traversed Washington's Olympic National Park there was never any dampening or muting. We got constant, unalloyed greens and we quickly – all of us – wearied of the hue and wryly inquired of nobody: When did the word come down, the decree, the commandment? Who promulgated the official dress code for the rainforest?

Attention:
Heed, you cedar and sitka spruce,
You bush and fern
Henceforth, be you alive or dead
(*It matters not*)
You must be clad in green
Choose your shade, your tint, hue
It's up to you
But green your garb must be!

Clearly the fiat had come down and as we coursed across the park, even that area designated the Hoh rainforest, I could see how faithfully it was being obeyed. The leaves on the trees were green though it was autumn, no fall colors here. The vines that climbed the trunks and swung among them were green. The bracken and cinnamon fern on trees and under were green. The mosses and grasses spread on the ground, green. Those were the live vegetation. And the dead? Logs of fallen trees with no life remaining within them were sprouting life anew, the lichen of green.

Actually, for a photographer, a landscape specialist, while it is initially thrilling to find himself surrounded by lush and insistent verdure, after the second day or surely the third, it gets old, very old.

In those first days I had taken over four hundred pictures. Not four hundred good ones. Of those maybe a handful. Maybe. Of really good ones, photographs I might one day be moved to include in a show or a book, I'd be lucky if there was one. I wouldn't know till I started working on images and not even then until some time passed and I looked over the keepers again and again. But even in my initial perusal, cataloging and keywording, I could not escape the truth – every single photograph shared the keyword *Green*. Enough was enough. The monotony would abate a bit if at least the hue-muting mists and fogs had been present but lacking those there remained simply green permeating, suffocating every shot, every scene. And it was not just me. My travel mates shared my vexation.

By the end, I would rate two – only two – of my images as worth printing. One was a scene that drew me, perhaps, because in it, the color green did not predominate. The grasses, like those favored by my artist friend, were well trampled and browned. Otherwise, the picture focused on a lone and mostly dead, apple tree, gnarled, bent but still, with reverence, I felt, pointing crookedly upward to its maker. On the spot that day I sketched a poem to accompany it when I assembled my next book of *Poetography*.

Reaching

One spring in the meadow one long ago year
Sap would not pulse through the old tree's core
Nor vernal buds of leaf appear
Nor sweetening blossoms; never more
Would romping child or browsing deer
Savor the fruit of its long ago store

Yet still it would stand, that derelict tree
Survivor no longer surviving, yet each
Passing season here it would be
Fingering upward as though to reach
To the Maker of trees, the Maker of me
What a lesson that patient tree has been teaching
I pray, my time come, I too will be
Still reaching, still reaching.

The other photograph I cherished from that Olympic visit was, itself, abundantly, tediously (given my curdled mindset of the moment) green. It was a waterfall tumbling down through green clothed trees, green mossed logs, green covered rocks, and green leafed bushes. Inasmuch as I liked the composition of the photo I solved my temporary aversion in a simple way. Today, on our dining room wall hangs that scene printed on canvas 24"x36", completely in black and white. I love it.

Now though, here in Georgia, my short-lived distaste dissolving, I write this heartfelt encomium to what has finally become my favorite color of all, the color of spring, the color of relaxation. (*Rest in the Green Room before the show*) the color of re-birth, the amplifier of bird-song, the drapery of dreams.

I think I'll print that waterfall picture again – this time in color.

PEOPLE ARE ANIMALS TOO

Whatever you may have heard over years, whatever feckless rumor may have infected your ear, the truth that I must pronounce is this: *I am not now and never have been Marlin Perkins.*

To be sure, he and I both played roles in television, I as a network correspondent and commentator, he as the pioneer television expositor of wildlife. His program, "Mutual of Omaha's Wild Kingdom" started in 1963 and ran for an astonishing 27 years. When it began, I was just starting my time with NBC News. When I retired from a quarter century with NBC, his show was still in original production. During all that time, he and I never crossed paths (though our mail often did.) Aside from television, the only thing we had in common was our surname. But for many people, that was enough to foster confusion, innocent viewers who suddenly spotted a face they figured belonged in a box but had somehow escaped, and, nonplused, approached me stammering in the attempt to make even tenuous contact. "Aren't you . . . Wait . . .*Perkins*, right, that's right *Perkins – Marlin Perkins*, I love all your animal shows."

And, unfortunately, it was also enough for my own friends, those fiendish painter and photographer travelmates who, aware of my being bothered by the frequent confusion of identities, plotted pranks. Thus, one day, years after dear Marlin had died and gone into perpetual reruns and YouTube, I would walk into the breakfast room at a motel in Torrey, Utah, and be cheerfully accosted by a well-cued waitress saying she just loved "all those wonderful wildlife programs you do" while the "friends" held up napkins to mask their snickering, my obvious annoyance guaranteeing that such sorry setups would keep happening.

It is not to such friends that I disclaim here but to the reader. If you, reader, do not know much about me, that's fine. But you ought to know a bit about that other Perkins for he was an American icon.

Born in Missouri, raised to become a zoologist, direct several zoos and then find his fame on TV, he offered what today would be considered a rude form of TV, technically unsophisticated, but so was much of TV those days. David Brinkley, co-hosting the famed nightly Huntley-Brinkley Report on NBC was seated on a stool at a simple draftsman's table in front of a background that was nothing more than a suspended sheet of unpainted plywood. That was all. Nothing more was needed.

So, if Marlin Perkins, seated by a sign conspicuously plugging the sponsor, made simplistic segues like "While Jim wrestles with that crocodile, if you find yourself wrestling with concerns about your family's future, Mutual of Omaha can help . . . " that, too, was okay. Nothing more was needed to convey the personal, credible presence of the man and the cause he came to represent, the cause of respecting and protecting wildlife. He was our first mass-media environmentalist.

One thing, though, was mostly missing from his programs: killing. On his shows we were not asked to watch an animal prey on another. Death struggles, we did not have to witness. Marlin sanitized nature for us. He was a gentle man.

(With a notable, small exception that came to be widely reported. A journalist once confronted him with the charges that Walt Disney in one of his films had faked a herd of lemmings leaping to their deaths off a cliff and asked Marlin if he faked his stuff too. Marlin, then in his seventies, politely asked that the camera be turned off, whereupon, it is said, he reached across the table and punched the reporter in the face.)

Mainly, though, he was a gentle man for whom nature was gentle.

Nature lost its gentleness when PBS came along with a series called simply "Nature." Created and hosted with erudition and so-phistication by a former NBC colleague of mine, George Page, the shows were weekly compilations of the most amazing animal films we had ever seen. And they were not sanitized. We were forced, in their exotic cinematography, to see (we wanted to turn aside but could never seem to do it) the brutalities that animals perpetrate on ani-mals, and, somehow, that forced us to make the connection that we, too, are animals, and capable of our own brutalities.

Another old TV show comes to mind. It was called *Animals are People Too.* Cute title for an amusing parade of animals cavorting. But I've always thought the inverse of that saying is more accurate: *People are animals too.*

People are animals and part of nature. Ardent, sometimes mono-maniacal animal "rights" activists seem to forget that truism or never accepted it in the first place. To them, Genesis is a seventies rock band; Dominion, what Canada used to be. Some of their leading lights, perhaps attempting to be controversial and succeeding, say things like this:

Christianity is our foe. If animal rights are to succeed, we must destroy the Judeo-Christian Religious tradition." That was the delivered wisdom of Princeton Professor of BioEthics, Peter Singer, founder of Animal Rights.

Whales have rights, these folks go to court to argue. Spotted owls and tiny snail darters, they say, have rights. Though, curiously, many of those same people think that babies in the womb have none. Without getting into those arguments, however, I find myself back to thinking about the human animal's penchant for brutality. Thinking especially about a single journey I made to a singular place. Another island, cold but otherwise quite different from any I have known be-fore or since.

꙳

St. Paul is the island, the Pribilofs, the island group and the word remote was invented for them. Hundreds of miles off mainland Alaska,
up above the scoop of the Aleutian islands but two hundred miles
from the nearest of those, the Pribilofs had been called by a Russian
Orthodox priest assigned to St. Paul "the land God forgot."

Seals didn't forget. Ultimately, they were the reason men came
here. Lore has it that an Aleut elder, lost paddling north to escape a
storm and then socked in by blanketing fogs which prevail in the area
found the islands only because he heard the bleating and honking of
tens of thousands of seals hauled out on an unseen shore: St. Paul.

In the eighteenth century, Russian sailors discovered the Pribilofs
and the alluring fact that thousands of northern fur seals come ashore
each summer to breed and have their pups. For men (Russians at
first, then Americans as America purchased Alaska) the annual hauling of the seals was irresistible because for many women, seal fur and
the coats and hats to be made from it were irresistible. To work what
became the annual seal "harvest," the Russians conscripted laborers,
willing or not, from up and down the Aleutian chain. Wives were
conscripted, too, to live in desolate bondage, deprived of any luxuries
and many necessities. The tiny Pribilofs suddenly had a human population, their lives and livelihoods completely bound to the "harvest."
("Harvest" being the preferred conscience-cleansing euphemism for
"kill.")

At the time of my visit, the Pribilofs are home to a few hundred
Aleuts, and millions – literally millions – of nesting seabirds. For
a bird watcher it is nonpareil. For a photographer, a boggling and
bountiful blessing. Producer Shad Northshield and I spend thrilling
and exhausting hours perched atop black, basaltic cliffs capturing
scenes few others – bird lovers or not – will ever have the chance to
experience. It is cold, windy and usually rainy. We lie on wet grass,
inching ever closer to the edge of the precipice that our cameras can
peer down at the mazes of nests clinging to crags and rock shelves

and flying to and from and among, flying over and above, the birds. There are murres, auks, auklets, kittiwakes, several sorts of gull, black guillemots, dancers of the air. There are gannets always looking so carefully groomed, nary a feather misplaced. There are several varieties of tern and then there are puffins.

Puffins! These, Shad calls the Comics. Just to look at them, you smile. Look at them longer, you laugh. You can't help it. They are proof, I've heard it said, that God has a sense of humor. They are tuxedoed little men with enormous gag masks on their faces. Their beaks are too big, their feet too far back on their bodies, good for diving, good for flying but awkward for walking about. A classic pose, making these comics even more comical, is to catch one head-on, his big beak sporting drooping mustaches – small fish he's taking to his nest for the kids. Both Shad and I burn a lot of film this day on these delightful creatures. He will include several of his shots in a photographic book he is preparing to be titled: "The People's Birds." He gets the phrase from a "crusty hunting guide" to whom he was praising the good work done by those who run the nation's Wildlife Refuge network, and the fellow tells him, "They better . . . Them's the People's Birds."

I don't agree with the fellow nor with Shad for planning to title his book with that phrase because I don't think they are the people's birds any more than we are the birds' people. To my thinking, we are all the creations and possessions of God.

I don't argue the point with my friend and we only have a couple of days to enjoy the cliffside photographing because, after all that is not the stated purpose of our coming to the Pribilofs even if it is the real reason.

The excuse given network executives to afford us our birding opportunity is that we are coming to produce a TV documentary on the seal hunt and the efforts by animal rights-ers to thwart it.

I am prejudiced. On this matter, my mind, as minds of others, has been poisoned by a picture. The photograph has been spread across many magazine ads showing, enlarged in stark black and white, the full-front face of a baby seal with – could it be? – don't we see the glint of a poignant tear in one of those oversized eyes? That that seal is a different species (harp seal) in a different place (Canada) does not assuage us. *Men club those baby harp seals to death!*

Here in the Pribilofs, men club the northern fur seals to death! Only adult, non-breeding males, yes. Not babies, no, but still . . . ! What can our documentary do to stop this? Anything? Our images will be powerful, maybe powerfully motivating toward change. That would be so gratifying!

Or would it? We will spend a week here on this story. A week is ample time for a mind – if open – to change.

It's a small place, the island of St. Paul. Forty square miles of cold, embracing as it does the frigid waters of the Bering Sea. Population is only about five hundred, mostly native people, Aleuts. Five hundred people versus, in season, five hundred thousand seals. The town has a store, a school, a bar, a waterfront, a post office and a church, the Russian Orthodox church of Saints Peter and Paul, a small building but for its bleak setting wonderfully ornate, bright green shingled roof atop its white clapboard, and all surmounted by the bright copper of a classic onion dome lifting its three armed cross into the foggy sky. We will meet the priest of this church, a sallow, black-bearded man in his robes of office filling a curious role in the seal hunt which is set to begin tomorrow morning. For now, though, we will be bedding down in the church's basement, grateful for the hospitality. Early abed as it will be a very early up tomorrow.

Early abed but not early asleep. Too many thoughts tumble and tear at slumber, questions insistent but unanswerable. How do I prepare for sights tomorrow I know will repulse me? I have never hunted, never had the interest nor the stomach for it. Don't mind being out before sunrise but for the purpose of taking the lives of animals? I don't need the meat and can't count it a sport. Not for me. A close friend is an artist with books about classic hunts by famous hunters in Africa and beyond. I admire his art but cannot warm to its re-sults. I'm more Marlin Perkins than George Page. And now, here in the Pribilofs, tomorrow morning I shall have to face what I will see as wanton brutality against pitiable creatures trying simply to have babies and rest before heading back into frigid waters. How will I be able to watch all the death without a piece of me, too, dying? Killing should not be a spectator sport.

Hypocrite! Listen to yourself, Jack, bemoaning the forthcoming slaughter. Do I decry the abattoir that gives me my burgers? No, but that I don't have to watch. As I said: Hypocrite!

Ardent young agents of HSUS, the Humane Society of the United States, are here on St. Paul for the week, pushing their campaign to end this annual slaughter. I should listen to them to reinforce myself.

I have one more ploy, developed ages ago in a bullring in Spain. A bullfight was the tourist thing to do and I was a tourist. Plus, the headliner that day was to be none other than El Cordobés, most famous and highest-paid torero of his day. When my buddy said "We *gotta* go," I agreed that we *hadda* though I dreaded the thought. So how would I handle it? I would take a lot of pictures. For three hours in the blanketing heat of a Spanish afternoon (our seats were *sol* not *sombre*) I took the camera from my eye only when a bull was not in the ring. I could watch the parade and various rituals and, of course, the intermissions without the reality-blurring interposition of a lens in front of one eye, the other eye closed. I would watch all of the bullfight except – the bullfight.

Will that camera-to-the-eye trick work tomorrow on the seal-killing fields of St. Paul?

Come morning, dawn doesn't so much break as continue. Summer nights are only six hours. It hardly gets dark this time of year. Days are rarely bright, more often, as this morning, thickly fogged and clouded, temperatures in the forties with high humidity. The best adjective for this morning, as most mornings, is *raw*.

We dress hurriedly and are driven the distance from town to the principal shore, the killing grounds where on this raw morning, winds at twenty tug at the mists rising from the beach, from the warmth of the hauled-out seals. They are big animals, especially the males who arrive first on the breeding grounds in spring and argue over the choice locations. The dark brown bulls weigh anywhere between four and six hundred pounds and each will have and jealously guard a harem of forty or fifty females, each a quarter the size of a male. Because these fur seals are so prized for their coats some scientist with nothing else to do – or a grant – took the trouble to count the number of hairs on a luxurious coat. 300,000 hairs on every square inch, we are told. And reciting statistics like this helps me on this morning to objectify the waiting victims of the slaughter I'm about to witness.

The objectification is made easier by my first survey of the scene. As far as I can see to my right and my left for the depth of this stretch of rock, grass and gravel – a mass, a vast moving mass of seals. A very thick, humpy, undulating carpet of seals. Pelagic creatures, they spend most of their days out to sea coming ashore each summer just for this occasion and when they come the sight of them all out here leaves me head-shaking numb. A half million of them? I can't argue.

And now, it is about to begin. Here come the hunters. I can't call them that. There's no hunting to be done here. Just selecting. Rules are that only adult males may be taken. ("Taken." Another soul-sopping word-dance.) The men given the "honor" of doing the "taking" enter the field, each with a long, stout and apparently heavy club in his hand. Women gather around the perimeter. Logistical support. And here, in the full ecclesiastical garb of his office, the town priest. What is to be his role? He carries a sheath housing what I'm informed is a ceremonial knife. For ... ?

As the first hunter approaches a massive male, I raise my camera to my eye.. It's bullfight time. My recollections of this day from here on will be snapshots, many wide angle.

XWS - (Extra Wide Shot) - The killing field. Viewing this wide, I don't distinguish individuals among the animals, either pinniped or human.

WS - A little closer I see the massive males, heads raised, pointed snouts upward, sniffing and puzzling.

MS - The lens accidentally finds one of the clubbers raising his weapon above the head of a bull seal, action frozen.

WS - The club has come down; the seal's head is slumped to the ground with the mass of his now unconscious body. (I've been told that as it is a privilege to be appointed one of the clubbers, it is a dishonor to require more than one blow to end the animal; actually, the blow only disables the beast. Next come the "bleeders" to drain the animal's lifeblood completing the kill.)

CU - The camera zooms in to a woman, moving from the edges of the field in toward carcasses. A bleeder?

XWS - Back wide, a tapestry of killing; many men with many clubs going about their business harvesting coats for women who will never have to see what I am trying my best not to see.

WS - What's happening up to the top of the frame?

WS - The priest moving amongst carcasses and doing – what?

ZOOM TO CU - He has that knife, that "ceremonial" blade unsheathed and he's . . . he's reaching down at each carcass and applying it . . . He's cutting something away at each fallen carcass. Seems to be placing things into a large leather pouch. What?

XWS - Extra wide again because this isn't working as intended. To be sure, I'm not seeing or having to see all the killing I know is going on all up and down the beach – My eyes are protected from the sights but nothing guards my ears from the sounds, the incessant, pounding paradiddles of clubs raining deadly blows on defenseless seals while other seals, alarmed and frightened squeal-grunt bellowing protestations. These fill my ears even as my nostrils fill with the death-stench in the morbid moistness all around. There is no protection from that, nor can I sufficiently describe it – Putrid! Rancid? Fetid? All of those -ids and more. Loathsome, emetic? Forget it. But I can't.

MS - The priest. PAN AND TILT - Let me find the priest.

CU - Oh, no! How can it be? Using that knife, that ceremonial and probably sanctified blade to vivisect, to remove surgically the male sex organ of the just-deceased beast.

"Collecting *oosiks*," confides a voice close to my ear. It's one of the HSUS fellows. He has seen me puzzling and figured correctly what has me flummoxed.

"Oosiks?" I echo, watching the priest deposit what he has just excised into his collection sack.

"It's part of the whole vulgar business. And it *is* a business. They sell those."

"Sell what?" I ask.

What I need to understand, says my cause-carrying confidant, is an anatomical curiosity about the northern fur seal. Not that species alone but many other mammals too. Humans are an exception. Most other mammals, as part of their standard-issue genitalia, have a penile bone. A bone running the length of their penises. Bears have them, cats, dogs, walruses, raccoons, otter, weasels and skunks and some primates like gorillas and chimpanzees although not elephants nor whales, porpoises, dolphins, ungulates or marsupials. Nor men. Men do not share the penile bone which scientists call *bacula*; singular, *baculum*. The word comes from Latin meaning cudgel or stick which, of course, reminds me of what the seal hunters are using to kill these beleaguered baculum bearers before me right now.

What, then, is *oosik?* Simply the word some Alaskan native people adopted instead of the scientific term. They know it as the bone implanted within the penis of the walrus, polar bear or seal they hunt and they have uses for it. For one thing, my companion tells me, when larger, fossilized oosiks are discovered, they might be carved to serve as handles for special knives.

"Like the one the priest is wielding right now?"

"Could be. That'd be some kind of sick justice don't you think?"

I have to ask. "You said you consider this all a vulgar business. How is it a business at all?"

"Priest sells them."

"Sells the oosiks? To whom?"

"Tourists. *'Come see the birds on our beautiful island and take home a penis bone.'* You don't even have to come here. You can get them mail order. Large ones can fetch hundreds, even thousands of dollars."

"You're right."

"What's that?"

"It *is* a vulgar business."

"And it's the church doing it. And all of us allowing it."

I go back to my camera, pretending pictures for what must be an hour, even more? And then, finally I can take no more. Our TV crew *have to* keep shooting, witnessing, recording the scene. I don't. And so, wearily, I wander away. I have seen more than enough already this day and avoided seeing so much else. I have been told about oosiks, been sickened by the sight of them being taken and don't intend to buy one. I have heard fervent arguments against this annual "hunt." But that's the only side I've heard. Over the coming days I need to listen to other voices. Like the people of St. Paul themselves and those who know them. I hitch a ride back to town as, behind me, the killing, screaming and de-penising continue.

The crew, producer and I have time over dinner to talk specifics – what shots we got today, what we need, whom we should set up for interviews, where to do them – the kind of logistics which, I believe, beyond being necessary elements of documentary production, serve me and I suspect my colleagues as well by distracting our minds from the terrible tableaux that today were forced upon all of our senses. Sights we still see; shrieking and clubbing sounds that echo, amplified; the feel, the very feel of death as, inadvertently, a hand touches the warm fur of a just-slaughtered bull seal; odors imprisoned in nostrils and somehow, as well, poisoning taste buds. We eat little this night. Where to start tomorrow?

Tomorrow becomes today. Today brings interviews around town. Not the outsiders voices are these, not the protestations of those who do not know, really know this place or these people. Who probably, even if they do know, do not credit the Pribilof citizens as truly sons and daughters of slavery. But look at history.

These people, these Aleuts as Russians named them, may have been descendants of the very first humans some fifteen thousand years ago to cross an ancient land bridge from Asia across to what would be America. Those who hung behind in the northern reaches, they became greatly skilled maritime hunters, their skin-covered kayaks skimming icy waters hunting all species of maritime mammals. In the eighteenth century, a Russian explorer, Gavriil Pribilof found the islands and the treasure of the teeming fur seal rookeries and the work began. Russians quickly began rounding up slaves to work seal hunts. The slaves were the Aleuts shanghaied from homes on other islands, ripped away from families, forced into indentured servitude. The sad cycle was begun. Over coming decades, then centuries, those Aleuts went from squashing poverty to times of being treated and compensated fairly and then back to scarce subsistence. This happened under first their Russian masters and then the equally cruel bureaucrats of American government once Alaska was bought by the United States. In truth, little acknowledged at the time of the purchase, the Pribilofs and their seals were the unheralded prizes of the purchase, profits from seal hunts soon enriching US Treasury coffers. Seward's Folly was not foolish.

For a while, under US control, Aleuts were well-treated, well-paid, but then suffocating paternalism set in. A far-off federal government cared about seals and profits but not much about people. Aleuts were made wards of Washington, reduced to privation and starvation, and, come 1942, shipped off to interment camps in abandoned fish canneries hundreds of miles away, in the same disgraceful way U.S. born Japanese-Americans were herded into camps across the west. Those Japanese-Americans got publicity and later small retribution. The Aleuts got nothing.

Returned, at last to their islands, they soon confronted another threat – environmentalists. Of this menace, one of the Aleut leaders wrote: "The seal harvest is presently a key element of our survival, thus any attempts to stop it through misdirected emotionalism of people who do not live with nature as closely as we do can only be viewed as violence against us and the seals."

That was the threat the people of St. Paul faced at the time of my visit.

I hear it from many. Interviewing locals today I hear them speak with ancestral pride and a touching faith in God, these stalwart people so beaten about by history, ignorance and greed. They are survivors needing once more to find the way to survive. If today's batch of environmentalists could think of these people as, truly, the sons and daughters of slavery and internment, might some hard hearts soften? Or do they soften only for animals non-human?

Is there not, can there not be balance? A skeptical reporter understands that an environmental organization is a big business and needs constant inflows of cash and it is much easier to pump-up contributions with magazine spreads and slick mail flier showing photographs of seals being clubbed than pictures of a hungry, unknown Aleut family in a place never heard of.

Cynical? Real. Our documentary will tell this side too.

We will shoot more of the "harvesting" tomorrow, wrap up our shooting of stand uppers and general scenics the day after, and hope when it's finished our film will bring a balance of thought to the oft-times fevered protestations surrounding seal hunting.

Before we leave here, though, I set aside one day for a special excursion I have in mind. One of the locals clued me in. A hundred years ago or so, there was a mysterious beaching of dozens of whales. Sick? Storm-washed? Not known. But their carcasses have been out there on that remote arctic beach most of a century. Ought to go see them.

And we do. Two of us with a borrowed Jeep and scribbled instructions head off to find a far corner of the island where, as we've been told to expect, the road, such as it was, ends and we set off on foot. Another two miles we hike along the rocky shoreline with nothing ahead but a calling promise. And then, rounding a bend we see the first of the massive cetacean boneyard. Skeleton after skeleton scattered on the sand and gravel, amidst tufts of overgrowing sedges and grasses. The bones have been bleached by decades of infrequent sun and eroded by lashing storms. I heft a vertebra. It is lighter than it should be but heavy enough to argue against my forming idea to haul one of these back to the States, back home. My colleague likes the thought but quickly compounds the difficulty of the task by saying, "even if we found a way to bring a couple of these home, we'd have to get one for Shad, too."

So, *three* heavy, cumbersome whale vertebrae we would have to carry – *How?* – from this rocky beach two miles back to the Jeep and only then head back to the town and eventually to a small aircraft – *If they will fit* – and then onto larger planes – *If they'll permit* –for flights back home. Each step will be challenging. The first arduous and exhausting if we can even figure how to do it.

Two men, three boulders of ancient bone, each the size of a footstool but far heavier. Doesn't sound like fun.

But, an idea. Not original but apt. Both my colleague and I have traveled lands afar where men or women (usually women) become beasts of burden hauling water or supplies or whatever by carry-poles over their shoulders. We need a carry-pole. The strewn skeletons offer plenty. We select one of the old whale rib bones about ten feet long, thread three vertebrae onto it like meat on a skewer, he grabs one end and I the other and off we go. It's a long trudge and slow, many stops to shift the burdens, but finally we see the Jeep in the distance, finally we wearily reach the Jeep, stow the three vertebrae, dump the rib bone and are on our way back to town.

Would be easier getting oosiks home as souvenirs; that would be easy even if explaining them wouldn't.

Today, as I write this, I can faithfully report that one of my prize remembrances is the ancient whale vertebra sitting out on our Florida patio. There is something about whales. For me, always has been.

CREATURES OF THE SEA

C *all me Ishmael.*
I can't help but recall that most memorable opening line of American literature as our small craft slides across icy Newfoundland waters in search of the elusive great whale. Not white, not this one, not Moby Dick, but a sperm whale it is nonetheless, still the greatest toothed whale in world seas, most ponderous predator on earth. All things considered, a monumental quarry to catch – if only as pixels on a memory card. We spotted him several minutes ago but were not close enough then to take our shots so now that he is back underwater we try to guess which way his undersea questing for the giant squid that are his species' prized food might take him. When again he will surface, where will it be? He can dive a mile deep and stay down an hour or longer, we know, but we are patient.

Our captain is not. He seems driven by something. Whereas literature's Ishmael served under a feverishly and fatally obsessed Captain, our Ahab I will generously describe simply as bizarre. (Legal revelations later will make clear how generous that appellation is.) Our Ahab – a scientist, he claims; a renowned authority on cetaceans, he avers – insists we head south. We photographers who are paying for the trip, intuit north. Why should we doubt Ahab? Because last night he dragooned us into listening to one of his scrambled lectures at the inn where we are staying (and which he owns) and we unanimously agreed that the man – scientist, authority or not – didn't make sense. So with him now arguing for us to head south and we determined to head north, he steers east, thinking we might not notice. We notice. He turns north. And we photographers settle in to watch and wait, eight expectant Ishmael's with long lenses in lieu of harpoons.

It is most of an hour of constantly scanning the horizon before we spot the great whale; sure enough it surfaces off *to the north* and we hear Ahab shout "See? Toldja," as he powers us speedily at first and than cautiously closer to the lolling whale. We claim our spots along the gunwales, lenses affixed, exposures checked, cameras ready.

There is bound to be disappointment seeing such a great creature as this on the surface. Mainly because you hardly see him, most of his mass – the sixty foot long body, the fifty tons of animal – lies below the waterline. I get shots to be sure but the shots don't get me. He moves some, swims some, rolls a bit but still, I'm photographing pieces. With underwater photogear I might be able to capture some Nat Geo-worthy shots but I am neither so equipped nor so inclined to go underwater with this huge killer. So from the surface, always jockeying for position with colleagues, I snap what I can get and wait. At some point the moment will come. The scene I await. The classic shot.

I figure it's a male. The females stay in lower latitudes farther south after mating and giving birth, the babies fed mother's milk not by suckling but by her shooting it through the waters into their mouths. This, while the male, leaving family behind, is off traveling the seven seas. In his lifetime of seventy years it is quite possible for him to range the entire world. Melville's Ahab had little chance to spy his leviathan nemesis a second time.

Our whale is moving. He rolls part way and expels something aft. He has just been feasting on squid (he can devour a ton of food a day) and needs now, I guess, to discharge. (Never saw that happen in *Moby Dick*, did we?) Photographers jockey to new positions on the rails; Ahab maneuvers to keep our craft steady with the animal, not too close, not drifting off too far. I keep shooting. And waiting.

And then! Raising his massive head – his head which comprises fully a third of his size and houses the largest brain ever known of any animal – the whale starts to roll, crashing that head down onto the water, down *into* the water, his muscled girth driving his body to follow, as, up into the air fly his massive flukes, sixteen feet across, tip to tip, showering us with saltwater sea. Shutters click rapid-fire as the beast powers his dive and with a final fluke-splash, is gone, the sea spreading his quiet, rippled farewell, his "footprint" as whalers call it. It is only a moment. But I know that even if my camera did not work, even if I got not a single usable shot, I have the picture. *Call me Ishmael,* and friends, I have me a whale.

Oh, one thing more, this a gentle lesson for a friend who wasn't with us on the trip but who later sees the canvas print of my favorite photograph from Newfoundland hanging on our living room wall. Flatteringly, she remarks the perfect timing, the coincidence of flying flukes, the shower of drops and, on the water surface that whimsical, floating patch of seaweed. All I can do it tell her softly, "Dear, that ain't seaweed."

Another time, another clime, Ishmael signs on with another *Pequod,* and this go-around gets even closer to his prey. So close I can pet it. And I do, over and over and over and over and over. (I think that's the right count.) There are, however, in this tale too, another couple of Ahabian malefactors.

This is back in my TV years, somewhere in the 35 years of broadcast journalism before I awaken to the truth that there are much greater stories to tell than the ones I am telling. Before I graduate from reporting the news to proclaiming the Good News.

The self-sought assignment this time is to *Laguna San Ignacio, Baja California Sur, Mexico* and this time Ishmael has to get there for himself, the rest of the crew, producer and cameramen, having gone on ahead. Hitch: Ishmael speaks no Spanish; the few citizens of San Ignacio, only pidgin English. Should be fun.

First, the challenge just to get to San Ignacio. A charter plane gets me as far as SGM, as international aviation authorities pretentiously label the narrow strip of pocked and weathered pavement at the unattended and rarely used field a few miles from the town of San Ignacio. What's going to get me from here into town, no people or vehicles in sight and the small plane is already taking off, leaving me sitting on my duffel bag, momentarily stuck and knowing not what to do.

Fortunately, I didn't forget to pack a bit of luck and before long up the road chugs a smoky old bus which I flag and clamber gratefully aboard. Going somewhere, it is, though I don't know where. The driver asks me something as I step on but I don't know what he says so I answer "San Jacinto" and am pleased to hear his responding "Si, Si." He looks at me expectantly before closing the door. I have no Mexican coins but a US dollar usually suffices in situations like these. He beams at the greenback, pockets it instead of putting it in his fare box and we are off.

San Jacinto isn't much of a town. A few hundred people and a waterfront. Most of the former seem gathered at the latter; I should be able to do this. With friendly smiles, cordial handshakes and my feeble fractured Spanish I try to explain my need to hire a boat ride out to the whale watch ship I can see anchored a few miles there across the bay. I get some head shakes or fingers pointing me to a colleague down the line at his boat but before long I get a couple of locals eager for the business and, haltingly, we agree to a price. Twenty American and they'll ferry me out to my friends on yonder ship. Fair enough. So I toss my bag onto their small fishing boat, they loose the lines and off we go. Isn't that easy?

For a while?

It will take about twenty minutes across, they say (I think.) And that's probably what it will take if they don't suddenly shut off the motor and let the boat drift while they say something that seems very important for me to understand. But what? They are trying to speak

English but don't speak English. I try to speak Spanish but don't speak Spanish. One phrase, though, they make clear and emphatic: *Mas dinero!*

More money? I am never much of a bargainer and in this case I readily recognize, my negotiating position is as solid as the water they might just dump me into. I am halfway between here and there and the boat is stopped and the boat is theirs. The twenty dollar ride, I soon understand, is going to cost a *hundred twenty*.

And is worth it! Not my money, of course, but even if it were it is so worth it! For years to come, one of my fondest memory moments will be from this trip. Many people I talk to will be taking home – often to far lands – vivid recollections of these whales gathered in this Mexican lagoon, pregnant mothers, mothers having just given birth to one ton sons or daughters which swim coddled, cuddled and cozy beside them. Those unattached and maternally hopeful females, meanwhile, are displaying their interest to the males around. Now and then a couple will agree and attach, often with a spare male helping secure the active male by nudging up on the other side of the female to press them together. Now that's ungrudging support from a loser.

These are the grey whales, shy of the size of the Sperm but still one of the larger species, adults forty feet long, weighing twenty-six tons. And if travelers have come a distance to see the whales, the whales have come even farther. As we see them now clustered close in this placid pool of the lagoon, they have just arrived from their long migration – probably the longest trek made each year by any mammal – from their feeding grounds up in the Arctic, all the way down the coast of Alaska and Canada and the United States and finally Mexico, their natal birthing and mating waters. Five thousand miles each way. Ten thousand mile round trip. They spend almost half their lives coming and going. (Many humans do too, but that's different.)

The lagoon comprises three areas. The upper is the shallowest and it is here the expectant mothers put themselves to give birth to one-ton babies. The middle lagoon is a bit deeper and is the transitional area where mothers and newborn begin moving about with other new families, learning a bit of socializing. Then to the deepest area of the lagoon populated with new families as well as males seeking mates and other animals enjoying being together. Here, in this sixteen mile long stretch, the babies exercise with longer and longer swims preparing themselves for their upcoming trek north.

Here, too, the tourists from the special-purpose cruise ships float by in small boats or inflatable Zodiac craft, cameras at the ready, capturing exciting scenes and tales for friends back in Idaho, Maine, Arkansas. Here, too, when time comes, floats a Zodiac that will bring pictures and stories to people all over the United States.

Our plan is to shoot a "standupper" of me in the foreground and a whale behind me as I wrap up our story. The driver moves us in close to a mother whale. She does not shy from our closeness. I am perched on the bow of the inflatable as we ease near enough that I can reach out my hand and touch the great animal's head. Fifty foot long, thirty-five tons, the whale could capsize us with a flip of a fluke but doesn't. Like most of the whales of San Ignacio Lagoon, she's a "friendly." She holds her position patiently as the camera rolls and I speak my piece only to hear the cameraman say, "Have to do it again, Jack, the boat bobbed in the middle." So we do it again, take two. And the boat bobbed. Take three, take four, and take five. All the while, that patiently posing great whale stays right where she is as I pet her magnificent head which feels like something most familiar to me. My own bald pate.

When living in Maine, we often got out on whale-watch boats to watch the finbacks (second largest of all whales, after the blue); the humpbacks sometimes called the clowns of whales, so great their fondness it seems for playing; and rarely a right whale, so-called because back in whaling days it was preferred, the "right" one to go after, harpoons at the ready. Frequently, too, we see the little minke whale, much smaller than the rest and etched in our olfactory memories because the good folks of College of the Atlantic once hauled a dead Minke out of the sea and up onto the shore of the small island on which we lived, leaving it there to decay and rot for month after month. That unpleasant time taught Mary Jo and me a profound, if crudely framed lesson: putrid Minke is stinky.

Now, though, with other passengers on board whichever whale watch ship it is, we thrill at each display of classic whale behaviors: the spy-hopping (whale sticking its head straight up in the air and looking around), tail extension (raising the tail into the air and holding it there for extended times; no explanation for this), pectoral slap (lifting one or both flippers and slapping them repeatedly on the water), tail lob (the tail flukes slapped repeatedly on the water), and spouting (the fountainous exhalation up through the blowhole; or as one comedian in his whale-watching routine puts it, "I paid two hundred bucks to have a whale blow its nose on me.") That last always gets screams of delight from whale watchers but their greatest applause and machine-gun shutter-clickings erupt when a whale breaches, hurling itself all the way out of the water, up and then crashing back down, doing that again and again, fifty tons of cavorting whale taking his explosive curtain call then submerging and invisibly swimming away.

And a boatload of humans who, combined, weigh less than the whale are left chattering in excited awe. Or, for those more pensive, reflecting on the majesty of one more of God's creations that some people still believe "just happened."

My first experience with whales – quite different it was – happened years before when we brought our kids from California to Florida to vacation with grandparents. Paw loved to drive us from their place in Punta Gorda up the coast to Gasparilla Island and the charming little seaside town of Boca Grande. Along the way, one time, just after crossing onto Gasparilla, we saw a disturbing sight. There, just off the road to our right was a cluster of sea animals beaching themselves, so it seemed, a pod of a couple dozen pushing themselves up onto the beach for no discernible reason. Some people had already waded into the water to see if they could help. One of them told us the animals were False Killer Whales, not really whales but cetaceans of the same order. For maybe an hour we joined the effort, pushing animals back into the sea whereupon they simply kept coming back ashore. And why were they beaching themselves? Nobody then or, as far as I know, ever after knew. Sometimes such beachings are due to illness or malfunctioning internal systems of the animals. But usually, the actual cause is never identified.

Years later, we learn of bottlenose dolphins beaching themselves on the sands of a lovely Caribbean island, and this time we know why though the explanation would be kept secret as much as possible. This was at the Caneel Bay resort on St. John, V.I.. It's early of a Sunday morning, most tourists sleeping in; we will be meeting at the dock to catch the first boat over to St. Thomas twenty minutes away. I make the boat but Mary Jo disappears so arriving in St. Thomas I immediately head back to Caneel, find her, and get the wonderful story.

She gets waylaid from her walk to the dock by the sight of resort workers out in the water surrounded by many dolphins, the workers trying to round them up one by one. Disregarding our rendezvous at the dock and not dressed for swimming, she nonetheless wades out to see if she can help. The dolphins, she is told, have been chased ashore by sharks, a group of which have been spotted just offshore. The workers, supervised by resort security, while not wanting to advertise the problem and worry guests who with daylight will be using these beaches, are trying to get the Dolphins one by one loaded onto boats to be taken into much deeper waters offshore well beyond the close-in sharks. She can help, they say thankfully, simply by holding one of the animals here while the boat takes others already put aboard to their destination offshore. Would she be willing?

Willing? To hold, stroke, console and comfort a wild dolphin? Clothing be damned, she wades out, water to her neck, and gently takes hold of a shivering creature.

Let me pause at this point to confess: we anthropomorphize. We ascribe to animals the feelings, emotions and reactions that are characteristic of humans. Scientists hate this and I don't care. I consider it natural and harmless. It helps me better empathize with animals, feel closer to them. I don't figure it causes harm. It's my way of acknowledging that I and wild animals are together in this. I don't own them; they don't own me. We are all creations of the same God.

So, anthropomorphizing, when Mary Jo talks of feeling the animal in her arms shivering, she takes it to be nervous, scared, so she speaks to it, softly, keeping up a quiet conversation, and he is comforted, she is sure. He cannot know the words but he can know the tone and gentle touch. His shivering abates and his pulse, beating hard and fast when first she touched him eases as she holds him, reassuringly. He knows she is a friend and is going to help. Somehow she is going to help. He trusts.

And rightly so. When a rescue boat returns, she guides him over to the transom deck where the workers lay out a makeshift cloth cradle and slide him onto it, hoisting him aboard. They ask her if she wants to come with him and, of course, she does. All the way out, she keeps talking to him and petting him, assuring him it's going to be okay. He is safe now.

They come to the spot offshore where the other dolphins were brought, tug on the cradle cloth and Jo gives the animal one last hug before he slides into the water to be quickly surrounded by his buddies who greet him, nuzzle him and they all swim away. But here is the moment Jo will never forget. As the distant dolphins frolic and cavort in their safe waters, one of them – and she is sure it is "hers" – breaks away and swims back to the boat, lays his head again on the transom deck fixing his dark eyes directly on hers. Is there a tear in his eye? He holds for just a moment, (a "thank you" moment?), then flips back into the water and rejoins his friends. She weeps softly on the way back to shore, shaking her head, thinking, *"I never knew dolphins cried."*

ECLIPSE

Why must there be mysteries? Why can't all know all? Why does a Supreme Being (and we don't even know that for sure, do we?) insist on secrets? Is it to challenge us? Or, if we accept the Bible literally, is it because Eve, ages past, encouraged her man – *the* man – to sample a fruit (that wasn't an apple though it is often said to have been such), and their tasting of that fruit denied them and us ever after any but limited rations of knowledge? Is our not *knowing* meant to leave us more inclined to *believe*? Is what we hear true, that if we knew all, absolutely all, there'd be no room for faith, hence, there have to be mysteries?

Whatever the truth, I do believe that our puzzling over natural mysteries can, if we permit, lead to profound revelations. And not just for us. Not just for us.

The mountain-high market town of Miahuatlán del Porforio Diaz, in the Mexican State of Oaxaca, was not expecting us.

Oh, the officials were. They knew. They knew we were coming and why. But the people, most of the ordinary villagers, Indians and native folk, had little knowledge of the army about to invade and even less of the reason. If told anything, they had been grotesquely misinformed by their own traditions and those who perpetuated the fiction that a monster would soon devour their sun, the source of their light and their warmth, the eternal nourisher of their crops, the coffee plants as well as the "Magic" mushrooms that occasionally attracted strange-looking visitors from afar who came in determined quest. Those were the curious visitors with whom the people of Miahuatlán were familiar. Not us. They didn't know and would not readily understand us. To them, we were the strangest of strangers. Why did we come? Why did we suddenly begin arriving, even *overrunning* their homelands?

We understood. We understood our invasion because we more civilized, so we loved to think ourselves and at least in some ways more informed people mostly understood the circling of our planet around the sun and how, on rare occasions, the moon, as it circles the earth, slides directly between it and the sun, blotting out daylight for a few moments. We took this as understandable, even predictable fact. With our species' characteristic pride and thoughtlessness, we seldom stopped to consider how many thousands of times humans had witnessed this phenomenon in awe and terror, how many absurd explanations were declared to be truth before someone figured out what was happening there in plain sight. (Aren't the greatest mysteries often those in plain sight?)

So the people of Miahuatlán were certain to be befuddled if not extremely frightened by the natural phenomenon they were about to witness, the like of which they had never seen. Even before the event, moreover, they were about to be overrun by an awesome army of strangers who, if they were coming for mushrooms sure came with lots of strange equipment to find them.

What the army was, in fact, were eight hundred scientists from fourteen nations toting tons of high-tech gear; those plus TV crews and satellite dishes joined by hundreds more of that curious breed of eclipse aficionados gathering from around the world because they knew what was about to happen.

That, of itself, was a miracle to me. Most news stories cannot be foretold. There's no way to know when and where they will happen. On the other hand, some events are totally predictable, even to the minute: the inauguration of a President; the dropping of the

Waterford Crystal Ball at Times Square; and that always breathtaking and awesome natural phenomenon, the solar eclipse. The event itself is precisely predictable and scientists using formulae beyond my comprehension can also report the best places from which to view the eclipse.

March 7, 1970, the best place would be outside the village of Miahuatlan.

NBC News planned to attempt three-hour live broadcast of the eclipse, something never before attempted let alone accomplished. It would be picked up by broadcast organizations of many nations. The broadcast would be anchored in New York. (Wherever a story was, New Yorkers being New Yorkers liked to run it from New York) and there would be teams of reporters and scientists in many places along the path of the impending eclipse. But the principal broadcast site would be there in the mountains of Mexico and that was where I would be, I and a gentle man and wise, Dr. John Eddy, astrogeophysicist from our government's High Altitude Observatory in Boulder, Colorado. He and I would be working side by side, he to tell the science, I to tell the story. And a powerful story it would be. Nature, God's instrument of continuing creation, knows power.

Our NBC team would be headed by a producer/director I admired greatly, a man with whom my wife and I frequently and happily socialized. He also was a veteran working around Mexico (and when it came to that country you didn't just work *in* Mexico, you always had to work *around* it, finding the shortcuts, proper or im- . He didn't hesitate to call on his many Mexican contacts for furtive favors and manipulations. Including the country's airlines.

His quiet arrangement with one of those was that when he needed to fly into Mexico, he would purchase, on the NBC's credit card, a first class ticket for himself and then turn it back to the airline which would downgrade him to coach letting him pocket the fare difference for himself. Then, when he got to the airport for departure, airline employees were instructed to bump him up to first class anyhow. I remember a time that I, having purchased a first class seat legitimately, was told I'd have to ride in coach because first class was full. Disgruntled, I boarded only to find sitting in what should have been my seat, my friend, smirking with no sign of regret that I was his victim.

Ah, but the man knew how to produce television, and this assignment needed him because it posed what in those days was a tremendous and nigh impossible technical challenge – a live broadcast from that remote corner of southwestern Mexico, a mile high, wooded and hot. If today such an extremely remote broadcast is near-commonplace, that is because of changes in technology and pioneers like my friend who showed the way.

The town was small, maybe five thousand people, many of them having never heard of an eclipse, let alone seen one. For them, the coming spectacle was likely to be frightening, alien, baffling. They would not be the first to be baffled. Ancient Greeks had been no less apprehensive; indeed, the word "eclipse" came from the ominous Greek phrase "I cease to exist." The indigenous tribes around Miahuatlan began a series of quite sensible, from their point of view, rituals and prayers to drive the approaching demon away.

That odd juxtaposition of mystified natives, intent astronomers and pioneer TV people flooding into their tiny town with bizarre equipment and fever-pitch excitement made the story more dramatic and the little village more stressed. Its one hotel was crammed. It was a no-star establishment to begin with and that posed special concerns for some of the invading foreigners. That there were no seats on the toilets caught some by surprise, but our intrepid producer, having flown in (first class) beforehand to reconnoiter and sensitive to what he assumed were our squeamish sensibilities, had us equipped. And so it was that NBC arrived at customs coming into Mexico lugging not just our bags (mine carrying two comforting jars of peanut butter against the prospect of dubious cuisine and its unpredictable gastric consequences.) but also, out there for all to see, unwrapped and quite unmistakable, three expense-account, BYO toilet seats.

The eclipse would be total along a narrow swath through parts of the United States and Canada so why were we and all the scientists and amateur astronomers clustering together in a remote part of Mexico? Because it was believed to have the best chance of clear weather and mountaintop viewing and longer time of totality – ideal eclipse-watching conditions. Accordingly, this phenomenon would probably prove to be the most intensely observed eclipse in history. Scientists would be studying its effects on everything from the behavior of animals in the Okefenokee Swamp way off in Georgia to whether the slight cooling would affect cloud formation.

In Oaxaca state, sociologists were fascinated by how the local people would react when the phenomenon they would not comprehend erased daylight.

My colleagues and I, meanwhile, were simply eager to know: Would this live TV thing, broadcasting from nowhere, really work?

We were excited, the scientists were excited, people across the United States were excited as Saturday, March 7 approached. *Time* magazine reported that a woman called the Hayden Planetarium to ask whether tickets were being sold for the eclipse. "No," replied Astronomer Kenneth Franklin, "it's being handled by an Independent Producer."

Historians knew that clay tablets from Syria told of a solar eclipse on March 5, 1223 BC. Even before that, the Chinese were recording eclipses four thousand years before Christ. In that sense, this was nothing new. Now, for many, it would be astonishingly new.

For the week we were in Miahuatlan preparing, the town echoed with a foreign language that was neither the local Indian dialect or Spanish. It was strange language with exotic words like *umbra, penumbra* and *antumbra; transits, occultations* and *syzygy.* (That last, one of my favorite words even before I had an idea what it meant; a favorite for the fact that it is one of only two words in English that are six or more letters long and contain no vowels; the other? Hint: Ira Gershwin said he had it.) Bantering enthusiastically in their exotic language, devout umbraphiles readied themselves for the magical three-minutes and twenty-eight seconds forthcoming.

It would take longer than that, of course, a slow show as the moon's shadow first started nibbling away the edge of the sun, then taking ever bigger bites. Dr. Eddy and I described and discussed what was happening, he in dispassionate scientific terminology, I in subjective and personal impressions. I was able to follow the eyes and gasps of Indians as the demon they had tried with incantations to hold at bay was ineluctably devouring the one thing they had always been able to count on, the daily passage across the sky of the sun.

It got eerie. Not just because of the frightened, uncomprehending gaping of the Indians, but also because the quality of the light, as it dimmed, grew surreal. I can't fully describe it; TV couldn't capture it; it was hauntingly unnatural, light not shining so much as rippling, quavering light-waves growing ever softer, dimmer, darker.

Efforts had been made to instruct locals not to look directly at the sun but they did. How could they not? Something was happening up there they did not understand and it frightened them. They had to look.

We visitors had been issued dark filter viewing glass, or could watch our TV monitors to see the dramatic sight of flares shooting out from the ring of the sun when finally began the moments of totality.

Then, it was even more eerie. There was light as I had never known light. Shadow bands pulsated and throbbed across the sky west to east, across the land. Time stopped. All was engulfed in shadowy timelessness as eyes absorbed sights they had never seen and likely would never again.

Finally – Totality! The moon's black disk totally covering the sun leaving only the brilliant silver ring, the corona, which is always there but obscured by the blinding blaze of the sun itself. The sun was positioned nearly straight overhead at its zenith and now there was no longer need to use darkened glass to gaze upon it. Now we could see it direct, the dancing ring of the corona. Now we could see that rare and precious sight.

And millions of people across the country, around the world, could see it too.

Dr. Eddy spoke scientifically; I barely spoke partly because I could barely speak and mainly out of the awareness that sometimes, words are superfluous.

How slowly the time of totality passed. Yet how instantly it was ended.

A sudden explosion of burning yellow brilliance burst at the edge of the black disk and the corona disappeared in it. The three minutes, twenty-eight seconds had elapsed, and I had planned what to do.

I stopped talking altogether. Even today, that seems hard for a broadcaster to do. To just be quiet.

I was happy to remain silent that day in Miahuatlan as finally, after the magical three minutes, twenty-eight seconds, the sun began its awesome reappearance, edging slowly – oh, so slowly – from behind the cast shadow of the moon. The diamond ring sparkled brilliantly, as umbraphiles speak of the first burst of direct sun after totality. Our cameras played from the sun continuing to emerge to the faces of scientists busy with their instruments or simply marveling at the moment themselves and natives with looks of awed relief that the eerie darkness was lifting, their sustaining sun coming home.

No narration was required, but up in New York our executive producer, a great Beatles fan, cued the perfect soundtrack. For the next three minutes or so, our broadcast was nothing but the dramatic pictures of the moon slowly sliding off the disc of the sun while, unseen, New York played the entire cut of George Harrison playing and singing his apt anthem: *"Here comes the sun."*

I watched and listened and cast frequent glances toward clusters of locals who had looked so profoundly distressed as their sun had been devoured and day turned into hideous and frightful darkness. The dark, I realized in those moments, can frighten, paralyze, eviscerate an empty soul. That fact – more than the powerful phenomenon of the eclipse itself – would haunt me.

DARK

Snow Road in Parma, Ohio, is where I learned to fear the dark. Pee Wee Hollow is where I came to love it.

I would take you to both places, tell both tales, but there's another story I have to tell first. This one takes precedence because it happened just moments ago. It was strange, passing strange.

I was lying on my bed. It was night. It was night and it was dark and that's what I found myself thinking about, even fixating on – the dark. I was thinking about the dark and though I was still awake, I was dreaming about the dark – a conscious dream.

I recognized the scene of the dream. I had seen it many times – the high ceiling, the tall and ornate windows, the rich mahogany of the judge's bench – though as I could tell now for the first time peering at it close up, it wasn't really mahogany, more like plywood covered with mahogany-print stick-on paper just as the supposed marble on the elaborate wall behind the judge was equally faux. The cameras never showed that.

It was Perry Mason's courtroom. Perhaps Jack McCoy's. Maybe both, come to think of it. Maybe they used the same courtroom set for both shows years apart. Neither of those well-known TV attorneys was present in my wake-dream. There were different lawyers, and as was quickly apparent, a considerably different case.

"All rise," recited the bailiff in his familiar command, "This honorable court is now in session, Judge Morton presiding."

(Morton? Hmmm.)

"Be seated," said the judge taking his place; he was a tall man, mostly bald, with a close-cut white beard. As though just testing his gavel, he tapped it gently. "Everybody ready? Prosecution?"

"Ready, your honor."

"Defense?"

"Defense is ready."

"Then let's get started. I see here," he said, reading, "the docket lists the matter at hand as the People . . . . " A puzzled look twisted the judge's face. Flustered, he addressed the bailiff, "Can this be right?"

"Uhhh, errr," the bailiff stammered with clear embarrassment, "Yes, sir. Yes sir, it is."

Quizzically, the judge read from the paper before him. "The case is cited as 'The People v. . . .the Dark?'"

"Yes, your honor."

"Extraordinary." He rubbed his hand thoughtfully over his bald pate. "Well, let's see what happens. Prosecution, you're up first."

"Thank you, your honor," said the prosecutor, a wild-haired thespian, flaunting a chalk-stripe suit from which bloomed a florid pocket silk. Striding dramatically toward the men and women in the jury box he suddenly stopped, straightened and spoke. "Ladies and gentlemen, let me begin as I shall conclude. With the simple truth which the prosecution intends herewith to prove. Nay, *shall* prove." His bass voice boomed theatrically. "*Dark . . . is . . . evil*. Nothing more complicated than that, Ladies and Gentlemen. Dark is evil; that is the sum of our charge and Prosecution will produce both testimony and evidence that will leave you with no doubt as to the proper verdict.

Stepping back to the prosecution table, he gathered up a half-dozen books, displaying them to the jury. "Start with evidence. I have here six different thesauri." Maybe some of the jurors don't know what that means, he thought, and so . . . "That is, thesauruses, you know. Volumes in which authorities in language compile official lists . . . "

"Objection," called the chief defense attorney. "Nothing makes those books or those lists "official."

"Sustained," ruled the judge, "Would the Defense care to re-word?"

"These volumes were put together by noted linguisticians – language experts – to specify not just what words mean but what are appropriate synonyms for words. Now, ladies and gentlemen, I have opened all six of these volumes to the same word. I pass the books along for you each to examine, and what you will find is that in each and every instance when the word considered is 'Evil' among the synonyms listed right along with 'vile,' 'nefarious,' or 'malevolent' is always the word 'Dark.' That, I submit, is authoritative evidence. Unarguable. *Dark is Evil.*"

"Your honor?" Defense again. "I submit that Prosecution's contention is *not at all* unarguable. In fact to argue it is precisely why we're here To argue it."

"You may argue but you won't prove," rejoined the Prosecutor.

"Gentlemen, address the court; don't start a kerfuffle between yourselves."

"Yes, your honor," and the Prosecutor picked up again. "It is common knowledge, common truth. You read books." He said it but surveying the jury wasn't sure many of them did. "How often do you see one of those novels starting off with the line – clichéd, to be sure, common – 'It was a dark and stormy night,' and reading something like that you know there's going to be a murder or something else dastardly and *Evil.*"

"And how about movies?" he continued. "How many screenplays start with the following writer's direction: *SCENE OPENS IN DARKNESS . . . SHADOWY FIGURES ENTER LEFT.* And another horror flick begins."

"That's how it goes, these days, in books, movies, TV shows – Dark itself becomes a character in the story. A character that always bodes evil. Fear, menace and fright, we are conditioned to realize, all lurk in Dark."

Fixing the jury with what he took to be his Stare of Conviction, he wheeled then and strode back to the prosecution table to scoop up one more volume, this one leather-bound with gilt-edged pages which he handled with seeming solemnity and walked toward the jury box.

"Ladies and gentlemen," he intoned, "the Bible. Many of you are Believers, Jewish or Christian. The Defense attorney, I know to be an Evangelical and so I'm sure he . . . "

"Objection, your honor. Strenuous objection. Prosecution has the right to examine the Bible if he wishes but not my own personal belief."

"I didn't know you were ashamed of it," the Prosecutor dug.

"Gentlemen, you were warned. I'll sustain the objection."

"Regardless," said the prosecutor to the jurors, "I offer the words of the Bible itself as what I trust you would agree is compelling testimony. Let's allow it to speak," and he began opening Post-It tabbed pages. "In the very first book of the Bible, the book of Genesis, we find the following: 'Abram fell into a deep sleep and a thick and dreadful darkness came over him.' Notice, it doesn't say a pleasant and cheering darkness but a 'dreadful' one. In the very next book, the Lord God through Moses placed a series of plagues against the Pharaoh and the land of Egypt, plagues of locusts and blood and frogs and the like, but the penultimate, climactic plague was the plague of Darkness, total dark covering the entire land except in the homes of the Israelites themselves. Darkness was used as punishment, as a plague. That, friends, is evil."

He paged to the next marker and read: "Dark is evil and it means death." So says this Holy Book. This from the story of the much tormented Job bemoaning his terrible life and saying, '...before I go to the place of no return, to the land of gloom and utter darkness.' Meaning death itself. Darkness equals death. That's what the Bible says."

"And that's what early Christians believed. Hundreds and hundreds of years ago, in the early days of Christianity, part of the liturgy of baptism called for the priest and people to turn toward the west and curse the devil. Why toward the west? Because that was where the sun set each day and darkness covered the land. Evil in Devil-caused darkness. So they believed back then."

During these past few moments, as he was speaking, something mystifying was happening to the courtroom itself. Its high ceilings were slowly lowering, its tall windows shrinking accordingly, the ornate mahogany bench morphing into a plain government issue metal desk with formica top. We weren't in Perry's or Jack's courtroom any longer. Where the great seal of the state had been on wall behind the judge there now hung a blackboard on which was written "Session Three." It was a high school classroom but the argument was proceeding.

" . . . risky gambit to use the Bible supposedly to prove your case. Because I intend to use it to refute, to argue the other side of this debate."

A high school debate tournament. I used to be in those, many, many years ago. Like the kid now directing his zeal toward an older man seated in the back of the room – the judge in this session I assumed, and the kid was tall and skinny, had short-cropped hair and wore horn-rimmed glasses.

I noticed the printing on the border around the blackboard: "Canton McKinley High School." That's where I met my future wife so many years ago, at a speech tournament there when I too was tall and skinny, had a butch haircut, wore horn-rimmed glasses and did debate.

"My opponent quoted Genesis. Let's go back to the very beginning of that book which of course is the account of the very beginning of everything. We're familiar with the words: 'In the beginning, God created the heavens and the earth. Now the earth was formless and empty, darkness was over the surface of the deep.' Darkness. Dark was part of the raw material from which God created everything. It was he who gave it its name: 'and the darkness, He called night.' So tell me, can we really say that what God used and named on that very first day of Creation was something evil. I say not."

Kid was doing well, I thought, and the man judging this round of the tournament, a tall man, mostly bald, close-cropped white beard, seemed vaguely to nod his head in approval.

Horn-Rims continued: "My opponent quoted from the book of Exodus, the Plague of Darkness. If he had looked a few chapters later he would have found this: '. . . Moses approached the thick darkness *where God was. . .*' Does my opponent, claiming that dark is evil really mean to tell us that God was inhabiting a place of evil? What was God doing there? Look in the book of Deuteronomy. 'God delivered the commandments out of the dark on the mount.' That's what he was doing, delivering to mankind nothing less than the Ten Commandments themselves. Delivered out of the dark.

"Later in the Bible, among the psalms is David's affirmation that, quote, 'Darkness is my closest friend.' Would David, one of the greatest figures in the entire Bible have evil as his closest friend. Of course not. Or look at Psalm 19. 'The heavens declare the glory of God; the skies proclaim the works of his hands. Day after day they pour forth speech; night after night they reveal knowledge.' See what I mean? Daylight gives us talk; the dark of night, knowledge. I'll take dark. And, in yet another Psalm, 91, this: "You will not fear the terror of night, nor the pestilence that stalks in the darkness."

I submit that my opponent's choice of introducing the Bible to prove his case has backfired. Dark is many things but dark is most certainly *not* evil. Thank you."

Kid had prepared. He took his seat to await the judge's decision. And in that instant, in that classroom, I knew something no one else did. I knew that this speech tournament was fixed even as the trial back in the courtroom was rigged. I knew because I was there – in both places; I was the judge in both places, slender, balding, close-cropped white beard. Horn-Rims debating the Negative was a younger I.

And the histrionic defense attorney back in the courtroom? Striking resemblance he bore to the grandly theatrical religion professor in college who taught me to read the Bible and memorize scripture, and kept me coming back to his classes until I had earned an unexpected major in religion.

And this whole little drama played out as I lay on my bed one night *in the dark* – the fecund and fruitful dark. Dark is given to that sort of mind-plumbing, mind-play. It is made for creativity. How many times has an author, composer or poet, stymied with a work, had inspiration strike in the dark of his room, hastily reaching for a pad (or iPad) on the bedside table to fix it before it fled?

Psychologists have long told us that the best time to find resolution is to lay the question or puzzle before the dark of our impending sleep. Then is the mind most receptive, the answer most likely to come, in the solitude of dark, far from the distractions of light. Even if it is not completely dark where we seek thoughtfulness, we close our eyes, creating our own dark.

Dark is what illumines that which I most I need to see. It brings to life evanescent thoughts obscured in the glare of life. It provides to me a sanctum for prayer. What better way to use a sleepless hour of night than to go to God and talk. *Here am I, Lord. I come to you in the nighttime, come to you in the dark. In the dark, unable to see with my eyes, I can better hear with my heart.*

The great apologist Oswald Chambers spoke of both literal and figurative dark when he asked: "Are you in the dark right now in your circumstances, or in your life with God? If so, then remain quiet. . . Don't talk to other people about it; don't read books to find out the reason for the darkness; just listen and obey. If you talk to other people, you cannot hear what God is saying. When you are in the dark, listen."

Since dark is the time to listen, not talk, I often find it best to indulge in the dark alone, with no other person, not even my wife. By myself I can lose myself in dark, snug it around me, huddle within it and wait, listening for a voice that only I will hear. Should I hear it,

I shall not respond. The voice will not need my spoken reply. It is no time to talk.

Knowing dark as I do, honoring it as I wish to do, I have to acknowledge that there's a tough bias to battle. Our own language works against us, our familiar phrases and maxims:

"I'm in the dark about that." Or "Don't leave me in the dark ... " Meaning ignorant. Dark should not equate with ignorance. Indeed, dark is the setting for battling ignorance by enhancing awareness and understanding.

We speak of "The Dark Ages," so named by the Roman scholar Plutarch who coined the phrase bemoaning the decline of Latin literature following the western fall of the Roman Empire. Indeed, those centuries marked times of declining moral values and religious conflict among orthodox Christians and Muslims, yet, at the same time, for individuals, they were notably times of growing faith and people seeking God, an irony that led many "intellectuals" to think such seeking – indeed, any form of religious pursuit – was itself a mark of the dark, a stigma our world has still not lost. It was the rise of science and reason that finally moved historians to declare a new "Age of Enlightenment." Enlightenment, good; dark, bad.

Compared to those Dark Ages, our times today are light and bright. Right? Our computers, cell phones and GPS's, our social media, e-Books and iTunes illuminate our age. Don't they?

Our morals, our politics and societal ethics – shamefully, those are shadowed. Technologically, we advance. Morally, we freefall. More closely each day do we fit the Apostle Paul's description of how it will be come the "end times." People will be lovers of themselves, lovers of money, boastful, proud, abusive, disobedient to their parents, ungrateful, unholy, without love, unforgiving, slanderous, without self-control, brutal, not lovers of the good, treacherous, rash, conceited, lovers of pleasure rather than lovers of God. Dark Age, indeed.

We used to speak in America of "Darkies." We called them that to demean them and given the persistently negative connotations of "dark" it did. (And still, in some hating minds, does.) Even the proper appellation, Negro, was rudely diminished into a slurring "nigger."

Prejudice springs from fear; fear, for some, hides in the dark. (Or the "Darkies."?) That should not indict the dark. For some people, shadows forebode. They need to ignore, not let the mind create chimeras to haunt the holy dark. There is, after all, an antidote. Bogeymen in the dark do not flee from light, but they do flee from faith.

Senses are keener in the dark. Honed by challenge, sight must excel its normal capabilities to penetrate the dark as best it can. Hearing is sharpened. How many times have you awakened in the dark in a strange bed – a friend's house, hotel, motel – by sounds you have heard, unfamiliar sounds that you did not hear in daytime but now, in dark, you did.

As senses are sharpened, so, too, is imagination and that can be a problem. A young boy I was, maybe five or six, when my parents drove my brother and me from our little hometown of Wooster, Ohio, up to the big city, Cleveland, to spend Christmas with our grandparents. Grandfather was a pipe smoker; the aroma of his sweet tobacco hovering over the electric train set on the living room floor, by the tree, meant Christmas to me.

It was a dark Christmas eve this year and our route as we neared Cleveland took us over what I would later know was Snow Road. Appropriate, for it was snowing heavily, the old Ford's headlights barely able to drill a narrow tunnel through the storm. From the back seat, Jim and I could not see to right or left but we could see and hear as Mom began jamming down her ghost brake pedal at the passenger seat while harping at Dad to "Be careful, Fred, be careful. Don't forget the cliff. There's a cliff just off the edge of the road here. A steep cliff. Slow down. I can't see." Imagining the horror of being hurled down that cliff, dashed to our deaths however many feet below, Jim and I froze. And imagined. Being unable to see, all we could do was imagine. Christmas eve. Monster cliff. Car tumbling over and over, down the precipice. Christmas eve, all of us dead. I could see it, I could feel it. No electric trains tomorrow. Damn the damnable dark!

It would be many years later, as an adult driving that same road heading to college in daylight, that finally I saw what my mother had meant. There was indeed a stretch along Snow Road in Parma where there was a very steep cliff right at the edge of the highway. What either she had failed to mention or what did not fit into my fearful imagining on that dark Christmas eve was that the cliff at the side of that road went *straight up*!

That one Christmas eve was all it took. I learned to fear the dark.

On the other hand, there were trips with Boy Scout Troop 61 out to Pee Wee Hollow where devoted Boy Scout leaders laid before hungry scouts a bountiful banquet of stars overhead. What a magnificent use of dark. Even in their multitude stars do not distract from the dark, they adorn it. They embroider it with lustrous needlepoint.

Ralph Waldo Emerson believed that such embroidery was the way to blessed solitude

...if a man would be alone, let him look at the stars. The rays that come from those heavenly worlds, will separate between him and what he touches. One might think the atmosphere was made transparent with this design, to give man, in the heavenly bodies, the perpetual presence of the sublime.

Mess kits are emptied, the food, always tasting better for being flavored with smoke and camaraderie. The campfire is contentedly reduced to embers and the hush of dark descends for one quiet moment. Then, here is the Scoutmaster starting the night's excitement. "Okay, fellows, look over here. We're looking for Cassiopeia tonight, okay? Here. Start with the Dipper."

"Big or Little," asks a young Boy Scout, maybe thirteen, eager kid, skinny with horn rimmed glasses and crewcut.

"Big-," says the scoutmaster, noticing a questioning look on another young scout this one new to the troop. "Have a question, Taggart?"

"Don't know how to find that Big Dipper thing."

"Okay, everybody, let's review. Taggart, follow my finger." He steps close to him extending his arm There are seven stars that are shaped like the bowl of a water dipper and it's handle. See where I'm pointing? There?"

"The handle's sort of curved? Bowl's aiming up?"

"Got it."

Beaming satisfaction lights the kid's face.

"Now," says the scoutmaster, "I want you to follow the line of those last two stars in the Dipper, follow them straight on. Go five times as far as between those last two stars, that direction, and you'll come to . . ."

"A real bright star, right?"

"Absolutely right. Actually a mass of stars but we see it as one very bright star. And what do we call it, scouts?"

Crewcut answers. "The North Star. Because it points due north."

"It is very close to the line of the celestial north pole," scoutmaster continues, all the scouts paying keen attention, "So if we stayed here all night . . .

"Let's do," says one scout. Others laugh, seconding the idea.

"If we did, and kept watching the sky, all the other stars would seem to revolve around it as that North Star remained stationary."

"But what does that have to do with Cassiopeia?" asks Taggart.

"Okay, so now follow the same line you took to get to the North star from the Dipper and go the same distance till you see a bright 'W' shaped group of stars and . . "

As the scoutmaster continues, every one of the scouts pays rapt attention. Nothing, it seems to the scoutmaster, transfixes the kids like the stars.

Stars are beacons of timelessness. "That North Star, Polaris, is 434 light years away," the scoutmaster is saying, "its light taking that long to reach us. We see the light of stars in *this* time, *our* time. But the stars we think we see may not even exist anymore. This is *our* time.

Their time, those stars we see, has already passed. Yet we see them and admire them."

"Will *we* be admired when our time has passed?" asks a scout leaping suddenly from astronomy to philosophy. The scoutmaster, ignoring the question that cannot be answered, moves on.

But the kid has posed one of the imponderables starlight hurls at us. By their light, stars reach us although we will never, in any way, reach them. It is a one-way transaction that humbles anyone susceptible to humility. Maybe, I think today, that is what makes country folk usually seem more humble. They can see the stars. City dwellers, mostly, can't, and in that inability they miss much. Skyscrapers hide skyscapes. In cities at night, reflected incandescence smirches starshine. Day or night, a city is filled with light. Sinatra sang that he wanted to "wake up in the city that never sleeps." He could have added, *and is never, ever dark.* Maybe it's just as well. Maybe city people prefer being their own stars.

I am no longer the Boy Scout, no longer the high school debater and never was a lawyer in court though I know the arguments and cannot escape them; they intrude in my morning devotionals. The Book of Job has God interrogating Job, asking, "Have you ever given orders to the morning, or shown the dawn its place that it might take the earth by the edges and shake the wicked out of it." The wicked of the dark.

Further along, God is said to demand of Job, "Have the gates of death been shown to you? Have you seen the gates of the deepest darkness?" Dark as death; death as dark.

Is it sacrilegious for me today to disagree? I think not. For if it was God who gave me the ability to think, including to think differently, then it cannot be an affront to Him if I do.

And I do. I think of the coming of dawn not as the shaking out of the wicked, not as a cleansing or escape from death but as a promise, an opening before my eyes of the hosts of shimmering possibilities the new day can bring. If —

If I renew my subscription. . .

RENEWING MY SUBSCRIPTION

One wakes in the morning a natural being, refreshed and empowered by the sleep of the night. The wisest minds of science cannot tell us fully *how* a night's sleep changes us but they know it *does*, recharging our batteries, replenishing the sources of our energy, rebuilding our cells and rearranging information in our brains. It is the nightly miracle without which we would be even more vulnerable to disease, exhaustion and premature aging. That is what God's gift of sleep somehow does for us, the natural man and woman.

But the n*atural being*, meaning the physical person, the carnal creation, is distinct from the *spiritual* being. At the moment of waking, we are not spiritual beings, assuredly not saints even if we were when we lay down the night before. Membership in sainthood is not permanent, irrevocable. Tenure is not guaranteed. It's not like being voted into a sports Hall of Fame and once enshrined then every day for the rest of your life you will be known and know yourself as a Hall of Famer, signing autographs to which you proudly append: "HOF". I've known some who do that. But that's football or basketball or baseball. It's not like that with Sainthood. Subscriptions expire. The world is full of lapsed saints. That I was a saint yesterday does not mean I am one today or will be tomorrow. To secure one's sainthood, each day one must make anew the commitment, take again the vows, lest the natural man within re-emerge to subdue and supplant the spiritual.

In the devotional collection of his writings, *My Utmost for His Highest*, Oswald Chambers asserts that what we need is *Continuous Conversion*. Quoting Jesus from the Gospel of Matthew, *unless you are converted and become as little children, you will by no means enter the kingdom of heaven*, Chambers explains that "Those words of our Lord refer to our *initial* conversion, but we should continue to turn to God as children, being *continuously converted* every day of our lives."

Let it start each dawn. Even before dawn.

The highest mountain on the Atlantic anywhere north of Brazil, is named Cadillac and is on the coast of Acadia National park in Maine. It rises only 1760 feet. There are mountains and there are mountains. But at certain times of year Cadillac has a singular distinction. It is where the morning sun first touches the U.S.

At four one morning I drove up its flanks and hiked to its peak with my large format camera gear to capture the moment. I could only hope that frequent fogs would not interfere and they did not. Horizontal bands of cloud appeared as a ladder ready for the sun to climb once it made its awaited appearance. I was not the only one waiting. Maybe two dozen tourists had made the trek for what they saw as an historic sighting.

It happened slowly, very slowly, the dark beginning to lighten, the change barely discernible. Then lighten more in such a way as to make it apparent at what point on the horizon the sun, in it's time, would burst forth. Between me and that point other watchers milled about, readying their small cameras with built-in flashes that would futilely try to avail against the far flung gloom. These folks were in and out of the line I needed for my shot but I could not ask them to move for me nor did I need to. I intended a long exposure and as photography works, in a prolonged an exposure – say a minute or two – if people in the foreground are constantly moving this way and that, they will likely not be seen in the shot. I have a photograph made by a master, Tillman Crane, inside Washington's Union Station. It is a glistening black-and-white of marble colonnade, gleaming floors, windows, fountain, ornate newsstand and – so it would seem – no people! "How could you ever get a shot with no people in that usually thronging terminal," I asked him. "What time of day did you do it?" He said: "Noon." And explained. It was a four minute exposure. People were moving in and out of the scene the entire time he was exposing but because none stayed fixed for more than a minute or so, they did not show. He called the technique his "People Filter."

And it worked for me that early morn atop Cadillac mountain. Not one of the milling tourists would show in my ninety-second exposure. What does show are the still-dark flanks of the mountain, their granite sloping the long way down to the sea. And the sea has started to come to life with the light of the sun which was beginning its ladder climb up cloud rungs. It is strange to be looking down at clouds as the perspective from the mountain suggests. There is much here that is strange. But, too, much that is poetically provocative.

Cadillac Sunrise
The clouds below are aglow
With the rose of the rise of the sun
I didn't come to Cadillac to be the first to see it
(Though that's why many come;
If there's a first, they want to *be* it)
Instead, it was because
There was something I had to get done
Alone:

To say hello to the glow
Of the rose of the rise of the sun
A salutation meant to make the newborn day my friend
For I believe that every day
Whose sunrise I attend –
I own

The question for its new owner: what shall I do with my new day? That will depend on how I see it..

Photographers know that if they picture a scene of, say, a tree in the foreground against snow clad mountains in the far distance through a wide angle lens those mountains will appear even farther away. On the other hand, if pictured through a long telephoto lens the whole scene will be compressed, shoved together, the mountains snugged to the tree. The lens makes the difference.

It is the same with the morning mind and the lens selected. There is the Worldly lens. I think of it as the GMA lens. If your first instinct on rising is to flip on TV (Better, to descend to the vernacular, you should *flip off* the TV) and leap headlong into *Good Morning America* or *The Today Show* or CNN or MSNBC, to be riddled by all the "news" they fire at you, then you have chosen the Worldly lens. It is a cheap and distorting lens and can profane the picture of your whole day.

On the other hand, there is the God lens. It is a precious lens, clean and clear and easy to use. If, upon rising you go immediately to prayer and scripture, devotion and contemplation – not delaying till you're lost in the pressing matters of the day that don't matter – you are likely to view the rest of the day through that same enhancing lens. Good way to see, to learn, to live.

FOCUS AND TRUST

In the beginning, God created.

I try feebly to re-create. Re-creation is my recreation, photography my excuse to be out in nature at every opportunity, presumably to make good photographs; really to make good. For a negative, yes, but a positive, too. Photography, I believe, teaches me lessons I need every day, lessons in focus and trust.

I go on treasure hunts, never knowing what I'm looking for which makes it more challenging. If I were outside, say, to play golf, I might happen past some singular sights but mostly I'd be seeing sand traps and water hazards or searching for my ball while muttering unseemly imprecations. I wouldn't see beauty. Carrying a camera, on the other hand, *makes* me see; that's why I'm there. With that mind-shift, reflections of scudding clouds on the surface of a placid pond are not a water hazard but a photograph-in-waiting. The synchronized dancing trees out of bounds will soon be in focus.

While finding treasures and carefully deciding how best to guide my camera to apprehend them, I am often doing something else as well, letting words – poetic words – tumble about in my mind, words that I think might enjoy playing with the pixels my camera is tumbling all to the same purpose: photographs and poems to praise the God who created all.

In photography, one needs to observe keenly, to see the beauties that are always around us but are usually ignored, passed by. In large format photography – the old-fashioned box camera, photographer ducking beneath the dark cloth to compose the image on the ground glass – there is plenty of time for the left-brain to be concentrating on photographic procedures while the creative right-brain can simply indulge and absorb.

I recall a moment in Maine. Noting a particularly dramatic sky, I quickly packed my camera gear in a waterproof seabag, took up my tripod, hopped in the kayak and paddled from island over to town. Dashing to a friend's place to borrow his car, I drove into the national park to Bubble Pond, a place I had wanted to photograph but the scene I pre-visualized (in Ansel Adam's term) required the background of a powerful sky. Finding it, I hastily began setting up my gear, fixing the optimum location for the tripod at the edge of the pond (one leg in fact in the water), taking the camera body out of its case and affixing it to the tripod, studying the scene to determine which lens to employ, attaching the lens, going beneath the cloth to compose the shot as displayed inverted on the glass, doing fine focusing, adding a filter to the lens to darken the sky, taking a light reading, determining where on Adams' Zone System to place the darkest values, where, the lightest, translating those choices to shutter speed and aperture, cocking the shutter, pulling the slide on the film holder, and only then, at last, making the exposure. That's what left brain was doing in those moments.

Right brain, meanwhile, was off in distant realms of quiet and contemplation. Left brain saw a pond embraced on both sides by rising hills covered with dark trees, the calm waters of the pond mirroring those hills and the dramatic cloud-adorned sky beyond.

Right brain, aware that our older son was soon to marry, played with a word and intuited connections that, back in the darkroom would coalesce into a little verse entitled simply: "A Pond, A Marriage."

At Bubble Pond the hills contain the lake, as nature wills
But look again: The waters of the lake contain the hills
I think this mutuality is what a marriage is;
No longer hers as only hers, his as only his.
Instead, once man and woman are as wife and husband
From then on each contains the other;
In each, the other is found

Thus did nature in those fertile days provide not only photographs (the negative) but insight (the positive.) Nature inspired. My recreation forwarded my re-creation.

A photographer I admire, DeWitt Jones, wrote about the spiritual aspect of photography in telling words, speaking about "God giving me photography so I could pray with my eyes." His *focus* is sharp.

He has *trust*. Photography teaches trust. Not so much these days when most picture-takers snap shots with their phones or simple snap-shooting cameras, all automated and needing no more human input than the tap of a finger. But in older days and even now with the more serious practitioners of the art of photography there is enormous knowledge required and significant trust. One must trust his equipment to do what he needs, and trust his own skills to enable it to do so. He must trust his maps and GPS device to get him to the spot to find the photographs he seeks. And he must trust himself, that he has learned its functions, maintained it properly, cleaned its sensor, and understood the unique capabilities of each of its lenses.

Trust. Not easy for most people. It doesn't seem natural and the question hardest to answer is simply this: Trust what? Trust whom? There are so many questions. Modern society conspires to keep us from answering those questions wisely by offering up false gods.

Our age of science and technology urges us to trust reason, hoping we'll forget that it is leaders of reason who take us to wars, scientists of reason whose creations pollute our water and air, reasonable doctors who learn how to extend life artificially and abort it prematurely without learning *when* to do either. Reason, by itself, should not be trusted.

Our age of celebrity-worship offers as paradigms famous voluptuaries who marry many times or never; have divorces, illegitimate children and palimony suits; use drugs, "get cured," publicly repent and, so doing, reap bountiful publicity; who commit escalating outrages of style, seeking attention, identity or both; who mount opulent entertainments as celebrations of themselves; who commission writers to compose their "autobiographies," full of stories they wish had happened. Trust them?

Our age of conformity, in which even nonconformists conform, wants us to tailor ourselves to peer patterns, though our peers, themselves, wish for change.

Our advertising age expects us to trust the lies its market research says we want to hear about products we don't need but will buy nonetheless.

Our computer age would have us place reliance on electronic tickles through silicon chips.

Our age of enshrouding bureaucracy wants us to trust government to do for us what we cannot afford, and it cannot do.

Our secular age presents doctors, counselors, and monomial talk-show hosts for our spiritual guidance.

Our liberated age proudly proclaims a parade of promiscuity although quiet surveys say most of us still honor marital fidelity.

Our material age offers a Theology of Acquisitiveness.

And all these — false prophets seeking profit — we are called upon to trust. And all these, in the end, we should not.

Ultimately, there is but one right thing to trust. It has many names, different aspects. Some call it Self. For now, think of it in terms of those soft, insightful murmurings of the unconscious mind which manifest themselves in epiphanies. Those, we must learn to trust. Bombarded by multifarious solicitations, lured by the urgencies of the world, we need to withdraw now and then to the solace and guidance of our own inner selves. Our own inner selves means that aspect of God that whether we acknowledge it or not resides within each of us. Trust Self.

Also important is trusting Others. This may be hardest. For some people it seems altogether unnatural. Doesn't society discourage our trusting of others by constantly casting up (newscasting up) the mendacities and evils of humankind as though to re-persuade us each evening that there is no one deserving our trust (save the newscaster? "Most trusted American," the survey tabbed Walter Cronkite years back.) We live in a miasma of mistrust, our doors triple locked and guns loaded, with X-ray's at airports, friskings at courthouses, windshield signs claiming "No Radio," vans pleading "Carries No Cash," parents forbidding leashed toddlers to respond to a stranger's avuncular greetings, plastic shoplifter tags clamped tight on store merchandise, cashiers demanding I.D. with travelers checks and phone number with credit cards, credit card customers cautiously pocketing carbons, detectives hired to spy on spouses, and schoolyards turned into chain-link prisons. Every day, in every town, burglar alarms on houses, on cars, wail our unwillingness to trust, our growing conviction that indeed we'd be fools to trust.

It is the supreme sadness of our time. If we totaled the squandered costs of security systems and theft insurance premiums, all the paranoid precautions, we would gasp at how costly our mistrust has become. And costly too in ways having nothing to do with money.

As long as you mistrust others you cannot truly trust yourself. Trust of others and trust of self are obverse and reverse of the same coin; each needs the other. Unable to trust our own impulses and the signs we are given to interpret, we will not trust anyone else. On the other hand, if we are inveterately distrustful of others, we'll be unable to trust in ourselves. What we need is a new Golden Rule: "Trust others precisely as you want to be trusted, and as you want to trust yourself."

Do you trust yourself as a judge of people? Do you trust your equanimity in trials, your ability to handle the insults and injuries that might befall? Only with such trust in yourself are you ready to trust others. Now, in order to trust others, you have to relinquish control (or acknowledge that you never had control), but the relinquishing is not a matter of blind faith. Rather, it is a matter of *seeing* faith. You *see* the possibility that sooner or later a check will bounce, a house be burgled, a trust be violated, and, seeing that, you accept. Why? Because you have decided that it is better to suffer a violation of trust now and then than the burden of mistrust forever. You are healthy.

BEARERS

There are two excursions involving photography, journeys flung far in distance and time that with years tend to merge in my mind. God has given the human mind that power, to bring together dissimilar impulses that really have nothing to do with each other, run them through its psychic blender and invite all who thirst to enjoy a draft of bracing elixir – in this case a potion with something to say, speaking of simple things, of animals and people and the roles each is assigned in the ongoing drama of life. Nothing more than that – and nothing *less*.

The first journey is by sail among the isles of Greece. The shipmates here are six friends and a sun-weathered Greek captain who knows his way and the ways of the island people and can assure us of reaching the next island in time to find convenient dockage. Further, if need be, he can guide us to a family's waterfront home where on a hastily fashioned outdoor table we will be served a seaside meal by the same woman we watched as we approached the island slinging against the rocks again and again the carcass of a dead octopus – tenderizing our main course.

It is a splendid week in trunks, T's, and broad-brimmed hats against the Aegean sun plus a generous slathering of SPF 50 for the outside, an occasional resort to Dramamine for the inside. There are some heavy weather days and I am left unconvinced that those acupressure wrist bands do anything but advertise one's proclivity to seasickness. Nighttime, at first, is a challenge for a six-foot-three novice sailor who has trouble mailing himself into the letter-slot berth to which he's assigned, only resolving his problem the second night and thereafter by sleeping out on deck, curious dockside passersby or not.

An early stop on our seafaring adventure is Epidaurus, on the Peloponnesian coast. Here, sky and sea wage a continual challenge of blues – which of them can display hues more vivid, more vibrant and intoxicating. It's always a tie of course since, in fact, one is a reflection of the other. We know of Epidaurus from guidebook perusal. We know of the magnificently preserved ancient amphitheater to be found here, an architectural relic probably constructed by Greeks in the fourth century B.C., expanded later by the Romans until it accommodated fifteen thousand people who no matter where they were seated could hear everything spoken on stage, so miraculous were the natural acoustics. Today it is theorized that the ancient builders happened across a brilliant technology – the banks of seats all limestone acting to absorb the low-frequency sounds of the crowd while amplifying high-frequency sounds from the stage. A fluke! If there are such things.

Docents on duty love to demonstrate the acoustics for us. What they do not love – and adamantly do not allow – is that I set up a tripod to make a photograph. "But, sir," I beseech, "as you can see, my camera (a 4x5 large format view camera) needs a tripod. One can't hand hold with this gear."

"But you sell," he insists and will not be talked out of his conviction that any photographer who needs to use a tripod is surely commercial and Greece doesn't want me making money off of its treasures. Unless I go to Athens and find the right bureaucrat in the appropriate bureaucracy and pay a fee to secure the proper license, "No pictures." Well, I've been to Athens – smoggy, smelly, congested, Type 'A' Athens, and no picture is worth suffering that place again. So, muttering something uncharitable, unchristian, about how Greece may once have given the world great philosophy and superb art but that was in millennia past; since then – feta, spanakopita, and insolvency. I forego photography.

At *that* site. But just a few miles down that very road I find even better, more original and inspiring photographs that welcome my camera *and tripod*. There's no one around except a few pigs wallowing and snorfling in the muddy barnyard beside an ancient and seemingly empty stone house. The pigs are not the picture. But scattered around that pig-yard are what at first strike me as large rocks cast aside but second look shows that they are much more than discarded rocks, They are history, stunningly ancient history. Likely as old as the forbidden amphitheater just foregone and these with no robotic functionary on guard to deny permission. Here is a fluted column section, fragment of a long-ago structure. There, other vestiges of capitals, pedestals? A dozen or more such architectural anachronisms stand or lie scattered among the pigs. Many were engraved ages ago, the writing in an earlier form of Greek that even a pastor among us, student of Greek, cannot decipher. They stand and lie about this unlikely site, tantalizing enigmas. Why? Why here, abandoned and unwanted? The dilemma does not yield to simple solution but intrigues the poet.

> *At the side of a road, apart, alone*
> *Stand columns and tablets of tired stone*
> *From an ancient and anomalous land*
> *Whose tongue we no more understand*
> *So I ask the gravers of ages past*
> *What seemed so important you felt it must last?*
> *What pronouncement so trenchant? What warning so dire?*
> *Whose greatness to outlast what funeral pyre?*
> *Were those etchings of marble intended to tell*
> *Of a hero who bested an agent of Hell?*
> *Or preserve for the ages tales of one*
> *Who rose like a star and set like a sun?*

If so, the vain contrived in vain
Through time, their lichened stones have lain
Untold in a moldering barnyard lot
The stones and they alike forgot
Vanity. Futility
Through the range of history
The world does not fondly hold
Its kings and warriors of old
Prophets and poets it puts aside
Neglecting whom once it glorified

Today we have forgot most all
Who once held lands and minds in thrall
Have forgot in spite of stones engraved
Most all save one
The One who saved

It is farther along, on the Greek island of Hydra, that I meet the first of the Bearers of which this chapter speaks. There is a scene that commands attention and nudges to life another poem.

Hydra, too, is ancient; there's evidence that people have been here for millennia but what moderns call progress has not progressed for many years. Stone-built structures, whitewashed by sun, are today as they were. No automobiles pollute the air or peace of the island. Only rubbish trucks are permitted to wind the narrow cobbled streets. They and bicycles, oh, and donkeys. By donkey is commerce committed, and that is fine with the two thousand islanders even when they are overrun in summer by thousands of tourists.

This is one of the islands our captain knows we must arrive by mid-day to get decent dock space so we are given the afternoon to explore antiquity by foot. The women of our group head to the waterfront shops. I climb a set of sunbleached stone stairs to an upper maze of cobble streets. I wander with no destination, no purpose but to find worthy use for the tripod and camera over my shoulder. I find it. Coming around a corner I see in the small plaza that opens before me two donkeys momentarily at rest, the baskets slung on either side still filled with freight to be delivered, but their master gone off somewhere, not in sight. It's a moment that can't last.

Were I working with a point-and-shoot or automatic, simple gear, it'd be easy. Snap! Done! But one of the pleasures of working with large format equipment and tripod is that it necessarily takes time. Usually, as I described earlier, that is a blessing. But with two donkeys, those stalwart and devoted bearers, standing side by side before a picturesque stone wall and their master no doubt soon to return and move them on, it is crash time. Trust instincts and habit. Get the camera slapped together and make a shot. There may be time after I have one frame exposed to go back and refine – if the subjects are still there.

Which they aren't. I get that first slapdash shot, but before I can refine technique and try for another, the donkeys are gone. The shot is gone. The moment has passed. Not until I can eventually get back home and process the film will I learn that the first – the only – image is dead-on though the poem incited by the scene is incomplete, its message still unfulfilled.

Bearers I

We are given, all of us, roles to play
We do not choose, we are chosen
The Director assigns each actor
Some to race
Some to plow
Some to guard
Some to soar, flying free
Some to lie by a fire and be petted
Some simply to bear the load . . .

And there, the poem trailed off, waiting, not to be finished until years later when I discovered bearers of quite a different sort far afield from a Mediterranean tourist island or any other tourist allure. This unforgiving barrenness is not a place one chooses for pleasure, nor do those living here have much choice. The region is called Turkana; the nation, Kenya; continent, Africa. Names mislead. This is not the Turkana of Lake Rudolf abounding in fish there in Kenya's northern extremity. It is not the Turkana of giraffe and zebra, oryx and gazelle, lion and cheetah. It is, however, that region of Turkana cited in geologic studies as a land of widespread deposits of gold. Does that sound inviting? It *sounds* inviting until you visit. Or are stuck here, not as visitors but as hard-scrabble survivors. Or, in my case, am set down in this bleakness by the vehicles of a relief organization bringing aid. Why should the people of gold fields need aid?

Let me draw a picture. It is a panorama of dry scrub and endless sand, right to left, near to far, a bleak. inhospitable prospect. At the moment, from where I stand, I see no gold or gold miners. I see not a soul save for a distant line of figures moving across the sand, sad silhouettes across the horizon. They move at a stately pace, these shadow-people, but who are they? What are they doing? And where is the gold in this gold country?

An aid worker explains. "The gold is all around."

"But I don't see it," I say, "don't see anyone working it."

"Yes, you do," he says, "those women off on the horizon are working it."

He tells. The gold is widespread indeed, but very scant. Very, very scant. The men of the area – and that includes any male child able to work whether seven or eight or older – are a distance away scratching and digging. They have done that for years although too many times they have dug down into the ground with the crudest of tools and reckless concern for safety and too many times their shafts and hand-dug tunnels have collapsed and men (and boys) have died. The aid worker says he will take us to the home of a woman whose husband was killed in a collapse and her son with him. Now her younger son still works the gold fields but on the surface only. She cannot afford to lose him. She can barely afford to keep him and a sister and herself alive. They all work one way or another. All day, every day. While men still dig, minor miners scratch. That is their mode of extraction. They scratch the sandy soil with the crudest of stone implements for any slivers or chips that *might* be found to contain even a particle of gold. They collect the diggings and scratchings gleaned over the hot day into baskets and that is where the village women come in.

There is no way around here to determine if there's anything of value in those baskets. There's no water here, placer mining is not possible. The nearest water is two miles away so while the men dig and boys scratch, the women hoist baskets filled with scratchings onto their heads and one after another move off in the stately parade I witness and photograph. It is very hot. I can't say insufferable because these people do suffer it, are suffering it, every day. And for what?

When finally they get to a source of the water two miles up, they will sluice the scratchings, separating out the tiniest flecks that appear to them to be gold. They will take their day's treasures to the booth of an Indian merchant who will weigh each slight pile of gold flecks and pay the women off. If it's been a good day he will give them just enough cooking oil and meal to feed their families for one more day. If it's not been a good day, eating must wait till tomorrow. That's the way of their lives. These dear and God-loved souls literally scratch out their meager subsistence from a few particles of the world's greatest symbol of wealth. They live an unconscionable irony.

Why do they stay? How can they go? They, too, are Bearers.

Bearers II

Not the worldly wise are these, but –
       Worldly wisdom, says the book, is foolishness
Not possessors of great possessions, but –
       Moth and rust destroy and thieves break in and steal

These have not wealth, but —
     Wealth is worthless in the day of wrath
These are the last, but —
     The last shall be first, Omega, Alpha

Wasn't it a small town carpenter, forsaking his laborer's tools
Who gave us The Way?
An itinerant tentmaker, homeless and plagued
Who offered the way to The Way?

Whatever burden be placed on me
I hope, O sainted tentmaker
I pray, O holy carpenter
That I, with grace, God-given grace
May simply bear the load

NATURE, MEAN

At times, for any of us, the load can be hard and heavy. Nature often does not seem our friend, appearing anything but beatific. If nature be the face of God, we wonder why is He mad at us?

I know what Emerson said. I agree with much of his wisdom but a line in his essay on nature in 1836, I contest. He wrote that *"Nature never wears a mean appearance."*

Really?

I write frequently in these pages about nature benign, a gentle presence offering bountiful blessings. It's time, I think, to turn to what Emerson claimed did not exist: nature mean. Nature frightening and destructive. Nature forcing upon us the question that has never been satisfactorily answered: *Why would a loving God allow these things to happen?*

That is one of the clichés of calamity. People's inability to solve the riddle that springs from our culture which assumes that there must be *someone* to blame for *everything*; that someone is always responsible; that accidents, and fortuities, do not exist and must not be admitted.

Hence that question: *Why would a loving God . . . ?*

How to answer? Should we try to soften our souls with scripture, reciting Paul's surprising advice to the Romans to "glory in our sufferings because we know that suffering produces perseverance; perseverance, character; and character, hope."

Even accepting the truth of that axiom, is it enough?

Why would a loving God . . . ?

To answer feebly as reporters on the second or third day post-disaster are prone to do, "It's this kind of catastrophe that brings out the best in people" is to duck. It may be true. It *is* true. But it is also unresponsive unless the argument being forwarded is that this is the reason disasters happen, to make us all feel sorry for victims so that those of us who act upon the grief by contribution or personal involvement may experience our "best" being brought forth. Without pretending to speak for the Holy One, I doubt that's His purpose.

A friend of mine, a pastor raised in a missionary family serving in India, notes that there is a significant difference in attitudes on matters like this between east and west. "Don't call it fatalism," he says, "or pre-destination. I don't want to get into those. But people of eastern nations are more accepting that such disasters are part of nature and nature is part of the world that God has given us; there doesn't have to be someone to blame." In other words, if God allows these things to happen, it is because they are all part of the nature he crafted and continually recrafts. Such is the eastern mindset.

Or as I would put it: *God makes not only sunrises, bird song and the perfume of the rose; He also makes nature, mean.*

Sometimes people help, unwittingly facilitating the meanness. Think of the shipping channel that people built straight into the city creating a clear path for hurricane Katrina's flood waters to inundate New Orleans' Ninth Ward. Think of the man-made levees that man did not make well. Elsewhere, consider people who stubbornly choose to live too close to waters that flood, coastlines that rampage.

There's an irony here: Usually, it seems, the people hit hardest by natural disasters are those with the least to lose. (Though their "least" may, in fact, be their *all*). Think of the people of low-lying coastal Bangladesh, lands drowned most every year but they stay. Where else to go? Think of the people of Haiti already victimized by decades of the impoverishing corruption of avaricious rulers, poor folk having already denuded most of their country's hillsides for the charcoal that produces 85% of the island's energy and there, in 2008 came four ferocious storms, one after another, and Haiti endured its worst devastation ever. Meteorologist Dr. Jeffrey Masters argues that, "in large part, these are not *natural* disasters–they are *human-caused* disasters."

Don't blame God. And as my India-born pastor friend notes, people in eastern nations mostly don't. They don't think to ascribe their loss to a Deity. In our culture, many do, assuming that God must be causative or at least complicit. So these self-pitying victims persist with their unanswerable question. *Why would a loving God . . .?* What else have they?

Well, if they are believers, they have prayer.

The Garret

What can we do when the word arrives
We were praying would never come?
Cloister ourselves in a sun-starved garret,
Hoarding the horror, refusing to share it?
The chances that we, alone, can bear it?
Slim!

Oh, yes, we may sequester ourselves in that garret, remote and
dim
But try as we will, we cannot secede
From life. Escape from some people, indeed
But let's not deny the one we need:
Him!

To Him repair. Everywhere
In Him to find our ease.
When evil grows ever more boisterous
We don't need a garret to cloister us
Don't need to go to our siren TV's
When crisis comes, rather, go to our knees.

To my knees I went on 9/11/01 and was not alone. For me, that morning had started outside our Florida island home dealing with intransigent bureaucrats. The cause being disputed is not relevant but the upshot was that, as a way to effect amelioration, as they called it, for a minor infraction (by our predecessors) and avoid exorbitant penalties, I must plant a half dozen five gallon mangrove plants in the shallow waters off our seawall. I must plant them and then photograph them every six months for five years so bureaucrats could confirm my compliance and keep track of the mandated mangroves. It was a petty matter, bothersome – and soon eclipsed. The two men were heading back to their county truck as radio and then TV began spreading the nightmare that would overshadow everything else in the world.

Mary Jo and I heard the first reports, just to the point of grasping the dimension of the attack and then turned off radios and TV. Details would be slow to come. There would be an overflow of conjecture, speculation, reiteration and re-reiteration. For the moment, those would be all TV talkers had to offer. It was time to communicate with Someone else.

Over coming days we determined to check in on the news but once a day, in the evening when they rounded it up. Not that it was easy to escape it during the day. Go to the grocery and a radio is blaring. Step into a store and someone has propped a bellowing TV on the checkout counter. No one wants to be without TV. We didn't want to be *with* it. Our only escape: Home. The garret. Luddites? Troglodytes? No, believers. Believers who knew Jesus' words from Mark's gospel: *Why are you fearful, O you of little faith?* The wise apologist, Oswald

Chambers spun that line to say "When we are afraid, the least we can do is pray to God." He said "Our trust is only in God to a certain point, then we turn back to the elementary panic-stricken prayers of those who do not even know God."

O, we of little faith, come to our wits' end not recognizing that our wits' end is God's wits' beginning.

We, the Fearful

We are living
We, the fearful, we the blessed
Since that moment we do not remember and cannot forget
In the righteousness of God
In the sinfulness of Man
Ever striving for the new
Ever clinging to the old
We are living

We are dying
We, the fearful, we the blessed
Since that moment we do not remember and cannot forget
In the righteousness of God
In the sinfulness of Man
Ever striving for the new
Ever clinging to the old
We are dying

The principal cause of death,
Is life
The principal cause of life
Is God

Why fearful?

By the way, I never did plant the six cans of mangrove plants outside our Florida home as government commanded. Instead – and make of this what you will – six months after 9/11, out by our dock, happy and thriving. were exactly six newly-sprouted mangrove bushes, generated without our intervention by nature itself. I sent a picture to the bureaucrats and never heard another word.

Since this chapter is titled *Nature, Mean,* a reader might carp that I haven't so far mentioned meanness in nature. But I have. For as 9/11 reminded us, people – even those criminally misguided creatures who planned and perpetrated the horrors of that day – are part of nature, too. They are perhaps even more heinous and despicable than the rest of God's creations because people have the means to know better. People, alone among all the animals, are given the ability to think, to understand, to accept or deny the God who created them and who gave them the free will to do so. Their maledictions and villainies are, thus, the most to be condemned.

But let me turn to examples of the more familiar non-human nature, the nature remarked not just by its meanness but, as well, by its fickleness, its maddening inscrutability. During the many years Mary Jo and I lived in Florida, hurricane-prone Florida, we were never hit. That would have been scrutable.

No, when time came for us to be struck by a hurricane, it was somewhere else completely and an awful surprise. This was in my years of television news. Usually, the business of news is telling other people's stories while trying to remain uninvolved and objective. Sometimes that isn't possible. Sometimes – rarely, but sometimes – the news gets personal. Hits home. Literally.

It was a presidential campaign year back in those lost and mourned days when a campaign year lasted only a year. We lived in Los Angeles but I was off dancing the quadrennial quadrille. Or don't think of it as a dance. Think of it as a hive of mad bees raging frantically from blossom to blossom, always buzzing. The bees I was hiving with took a break, alighting in Washington for a weekend. Weary from too many of the same speeches and doing too many of the same stories about the same speeches I chose to hole up in a room in the soon-to-be-notorious Watergate and order a sumptuous wheelaway repast, cozy and safe against lashing rains outside.

After my meal and a few chapters in the book *du jour* I flipped on the TV to find folks talking about the weather, saying that those rains out there, slashing and smacking at my window were something more than beatific summer waterings. They were torrents of a magnitude rarely known thereabouts, rivering streets and rampaging local streams, persistently, drenchingly creating a flood that would prove to be a flood like none other in these parts. That's what TV was saying and you had to believe it because they weren't saying it on a regular newscast; they were pre-empting the *Tonight Show*. It had to be serious.

"Authorities in Virginia announce that there is a danger now to the Barcroft Dam. The lake there is so swollen it threatens to flow over the top of the dam and the dam seems to be in weakened condition. There's a risk of its being breached." So said the man on TV – much as I might have said it, objectively, dispassionately, uninvolved.

But that particular evening, I was not *saying*, I was *hearing* and rather than being objective, dispassionate or uninvolved, I was thunderstruck. *The Barcroft Dam threatened? That meant our old home was threatened.*

It was the home we loved so much during our time there, the first home Jo and I had ever owned, that when we found ourselves being transferred from Washington to Hong Kong, we chose to keep the Lake Barcroft house and lease it out to friends. Should we ever return to the area, that house on the shore of a placid lake just twenty minutes from the nation's capitol and next to our dear neighbors, Ann and Freemie Williams, was the only place we would want to live.

I need to explain the topography. Lake Barcroft, a two-mile long lake fed by two branches of a stream called Holmes Run, comprised two long fingers of clear water that merged to move gently down toward our end where a concrete dam retained the water. The dam stretched four hundred feet end to end and rose sixty-eight feet above the stream bed below. From there the tamed waters flowed toward the town of Alexandria. Indeed, the lake had been envisioned by George Washington to serve as a reservoir for Alexandria and in 1913 it was built for that purpose, holding some 800,000,000 gallons of fresh water. Eventually, even that was not enough for a growing Alexandria which developed other sources and the lake became the centerpiece of a thriving community of water-lovers taking eager use of its recreational opportunities, sailing, canoeing, fishing, gliding across its 135 acres in electric-powered picnic barges, (no gasoline engines permitted). Rimming the lake were approximately a thousand homes of people who enjoyed a very felicitous lifestyle.

The one other thing I need to say about the dam, though, is that at its western end, its concrete structure embedded itself hard into the side of a hill that climbed in terraces thirty-five feet. That hill was our back yard! Our house sat atop the hill, looking down on the lake to the left of the dam, the woods dropping down to the stream to the right. Our lawn, the left part of it, stepped down to water's edge, a small sand beach, and a weeping willow we had planted to honor the birth of our first child, Mark Christopher. The Topher tree. A rope hammock was slung between another tree and an upright railroad tie sunk in the ground. The Williamses with their dock and party barge were immediately to our left, our properties adjoining, our doors always open to each other, neighbors always welcome. On the wall behind Freemie's basement bar was a photograph of the two of us that I had signed "To My Best Neighbor By A Dam Site!" We loved the Williamses; we loved the home; we loved Lake Barcroft. What was happening to it? What was happening to the dam? Because as I understood too painfully, what happened to the dam happened to us.

"Authorities now report that the danger to the Barcroft dam in suburban Virginia has passed. There is no longer any danger to the Barcroft dam."

It was 1:15 a.m. and those words from the TV gave me solace. I went to bed. Tomorrow I'd call Ann and Freemie and see what the heck was happening out there.

By morning the storm had mostly abated but TV reported it had indeed been a singular event. Heaviest rains recorded in the area in 125 years. Nor was it an isolated downpour, but the drenching outer bands of a full-fledged hurricane, a storm named Agnes, it being the first of the season. For the area around Washington, reporters were saying, it had been the Storm of the Century. Ah, but you know how TV folks hyperbolize!

I phoned the Williamses and as soon as they knew who it was, they were both in tears, loudly weeping so that I had trouble understanding what they were trying to tell me. When I understood, I realized they were not crying for themselves but for me.

"Your house," Ann got out between sobs and sniffles, "can't make it! . . . yard's gone . . . whole thing . . . whole hillside . . . washed away . . . no more lake . . . lake's gone . . . terrible! . . . Oh, Jack, so terrible . . . sorry . . . sorry . . . "

Lake's gone? Come on. A two-mile long lake couldn't be *gone!*. Panicked, Ann must be severely exaggerating. But Freemie hadn't disagreed with her and Colonel Freeman Williams, former Marine pilot, Q. B., Ramblin' Wreck from Georgia Tech, wasn't a man who severely exaggerated. Still, how could the lake be gone? Where could it go? Had the dam given way? TV had said the dam was out of danger. What they hadn't explained was why.

"I'll be right out." Grabbing a rental car, I hit the familiar road, across the bridge, past the Pentagon, out Columbia Pike, beyond Bailey's Crossroads, turning into the Barcroft community and onto Lakeview Drive which I was stunned to realize no longer had a lake view – because, indeed, *there was no more lake!*

The paragraph that follows understates my reaction as I approached our house and saw what I saw. It understates because there aren't words. A hammering, a slugging, a psychic convulsion, a time when there is no shame in weeping and no perceived need for civility.

A reporter approached asking if I'd mind posing by the house. I didn't answer. Somebody came up to say how awful it was. I walked away. "What do you think, Mr. Perkins?" asked another reporter sticking a microphone in my face. And I blew. "Go away. *Just. Go. Away.*"

Pushing past him I walked toward the backyard … toward where the back yard should have been and finally I saw. I saw, I saw, I saw, and still could not comprehend. Turning away I blindly aimed for Freemie's garage, into their house, down to the basement, over to the bar and – sonofabitch! – he had it locked. I got glass and ice and mix but the vodka was battened. So sit there. Try to understand the plight you're in, young Land Baron.

Nothing there! The entire back yard, the hillside sloping down to the lake, the beach, the trees and terraces and patio – THE WHOLE HILL, washed away, the house, teetering atop a fifty foot precipice, its foundation nakedly exposed. How could it stand? Could it stand?

The Williamses having not yet returned, I walked down into what had been the lake; I saw only a small puddle out at the deepest point. All that was left of Lake Barcroft.

"Jack!" Ann and Freeman had returned along with the Mastersons, our displaced tenants.

"Freemie, first question: mind unlocking the vodka?"

We sat with Bloody Marys as, together, words tumbling over each other, they told me the story.

As rains pelted last night, the lake started rising. At first, their concern was that it might wash up onto the lower level of their yard. That, and Freemie's party barge. He went out in the rain and secured it more tightly. But as they watched the lake continuing to rise throughout the evening, those concerns seemed inconsequential. It rose all the way up to the flood gates of the dam which were not opened. Operators of the dam years earlier had cemented most of the flood gates permanently closed, afraid that if they were ever opened they might flood properties downstream. As it turned out, by *not opening them* they flooded properties downstream even worse. (As I wrote earlier, sometimes people facilitate nature's meanness.)

The lake, while overflowing the dam, also began probing around the end of the dam, our end, at first trickling and then flowing, and then gushing, and then ripping away loose beach soil, running and washing, lifting out a small hemlock and another and another, running and washing; faster, with more force and more fury waters ran and washed and dug, spray flashing to the sky, waters raging in the dark. The Topher tree went. It had grown to twenty feet tall; it went. I was told that Grandad went only minutes thereafter. Oaks are made to rule as eucalyptus are made to perfume. Grandad was a fulsome majesty of oak, ten feet thick at the trunk, a hundred feet high. Its roots must have spread for a quarter acre. What a sight it must have been to see him go. What furious waters they must have been to take Grandad. What became of the animals and birds that lived in him?

The Mastersons picked up: They had stood in the lake-facing living room window as long as they dared, awe-struck by the spectacle below them, but when the picnic table on the uppermost yard patio suddenly dropped from view, the earth beneath it undermined and collapsed, they abandoned, taking hurried refuge next door.

It had taken an hour, no more, from the moment the waters began gouging away our land until it had excavated all the back to the foundations of our house, stopping only when, hitting bed rock beneath our house it could excavate no more. By then it had disgorged every one of the lake's eight hundred million gallons of water

It was midnight. As the TV folk would report, the danger to the Barcroft dam had passed. Now I knew why. The dam didn't give way because our back yard did.

Friends consoled. One said "Don't worry, Jack, you'll end up all right." I didn't believe it. If the house did not fall from further erosion into the new canyon beneath it, at the very least, we would never be able to afford to engineer a wall up the cliff to support it, let alone restore the hill which had gone. The tenants were moving out and here came a guy from the County Engineer's office putting up signs in our front yard declaring; *This House Is Unsafe For Human Occupancy.*

I found the reporter I'd yelled at, apologized and told him, sure, if he wanted, he could take a picture.

I called Mary Price, our realtor and insurance agent and asked her to check if we were covered. She said she already had; since we had no flood insurance, we weren't.

I drove back to the Watergate, ordered dinner and, calling Mary Jo out in California, tried to explain what had happened and what it looked like but found myself, uncharacteristically, wordless.

Next morning, my problem was solved. Both the *Washington Post* and the *Evening Star* led their storm wrapup with the photo of me in the empty lakebed looking up at house so precariously perched at the top of the brand-new cliff. By the time I called Jo again, she'd seen it in the L.A papers. Now she knew.

The picture ran in many papers, many cities. I heard from friends far-flung and spent that Saturday as I had spent so many sweet Saturdays in years past, with Ann and Freemie.

Freemie had been figuring. The proud Ramblin' Wreck had hauled out his "slipstick" (slide rule) and calculated. Eyeballing the size of the new gorge, depth, breadth, width, he figured that no less than one million tons of earth had been ripped out of our back yard. One million tons of earth. In about an hour. What a monstrous disembowelment!

Engineers and officials of the Lake Barcroft homeowners association came by. Dwight Dodd came by. He was the man who had built our house. His inspection now was encouraging. Place looked structurally secure. He stressed the crucial importance of the geometry: By the time the water had eroded *back* to where the house would be the next thing to go, it had also eroded *down* to bedrock which stopped any further erosion. Just in time! That close!

Engineers visited. County, Army Corps, and then the men from a Baltimore consultancy firm that would start sketching out plans to restore the lake. It had already been agreed by the owners of lakeside homes that they needed their lake. Whatever it took.

I thought of Freemie's calcuiation. If one million tons of earth was gouged away, one million tons of earth would have to be replaced. A large dirt hauling truck holds ten cubic yards which is twenty tons. So it would take fifty-thousand truckloads to rebuild our backyard and permit the lake to refill. Freemie kept figuring. If they could get an efficient shuttle operation running, say one truck pulling down the Williams' driveway, across our side yard to dump another load of dirt over the precipice every five minutes of every working hour of every working day, it would take two years to complete the job. Two years for men and their machines to undo what nature mean had done in one hour!

Lake Barcroft homeowners came up with a possible solution: asking Washington for a multi-million-dollar loan. The Federal government had announced it intended to disburse $2.2 billion in hurricane relief – alms to the downtrodden, succor for the sad, manna from the national monuments, and suddenly the only thing that counted was to make sure you got your share. Don't call it selfish or avaricious, call it pragmatic, they told me.

Alas, though, the Homeowners Association, an admittedly well-off group generally, hesitated at accepting relief, anticipating how the news media might portray it. So instead of an organization fronting for the privileged residents of a private lake community filing for federal assistance, the suggestion was advanced that the plea should come from each homeowner who had been directly affected.

Of which there was one. I — neighbors concluded — should submit the paperwork to petition the taxpayers to give me a disaster loan of however many millions of dollars, so our property, their property and the lake itself could be restored. Their reasoning lost me in a fog of chatter about loan forgiveness and low interest and guaranteeing repayment, because I couldn't get past the number. More than a million dollars?

I called Mary Jo. A wise woman, her only question was, "What would our monthly payments be?"

Next day, as the campaign and I dipped into Florida, I spotted a headline on the *Fort Myers Times*:

Agnes Disaster of Year — 118 Lives, $3 Billion Lost

It put things in perspective. We had not lost life. Plus which, to have been smashed by a trivial disaster would have been pitiful, but to have been singled out by a major hurricane and still be alive and kicking is something to celebrate.

My next time back in the capital, the Williamses gathered a few friends in their yard. Drinks and commiseration. One of the guests was their priest, a red-faced cherub who enjoyed a cocktail. Noting how a headline I'd seen described the storm I asked him what he thought it should be called, he said "A dam disaster." Then he remembered the name of our builder and added, "A Dodd dam disaster."

"You said it, Father," I responded.

"No, I didn't," he insisted.

It would take a long while — many, many sessions with lawyers, government agencies, bureaucrats, insurance companies and neighbors but eventually our back hill would be restored, the dam reconstructed (with flood gates that were *not* cemented shut), our house secured and quickly sold.

It worked out. For those of faith, it seems things usually do. Either things work out or people adapt and accept. God enables both.

Oh, and once more, we didn't have to plant mangroves.

NATURE, MEANEST

Beyond hurricanes, what is the meanest of all the acts of nature? As a onetime Angeleño and two time victim, I cast a survivor's vote for earthquake. (Note: Throughout these paragraphs the reader should appreciate that I shall not once use the word "temblor." No one does except broadcasters compelled by a mistaken notion given them by a pedant professor somewhere that it is important, to avoid monotony in your writing, to not use the same word repeatedly when appropriate synonyms are available. Hence, after a couple times employing the words *earthquake* and *quake*, the gullible journalist, to flaunt his schooling and his thesaurus, turns to *temblor*. Like a weather woman starts speaking of how many inches we can expect tonight of "The white stuff." Thank goodness when reporting rain she never gets around to talking of "the wet stuff.")

My argument for earthquakes as the meanest of nature's assaults reduces to this. In most every other natural disaster where do we seek refuge? The earth. Tornado? Go to the storm cellar. Hurricane? Inside ground floor or below. Caught outside by lightning? Find a gully, hug the ground. Inescapable wildfire? Basement. What about unnatural threats? Wartime attacks, bombings, strafing, missiles. Go underground. Natural or man made disasters, seek safety low. As low as we can get. In the ground itself if possible. Our ultimate refuge is the earth. Solid ground. *Terra firma.*

Until suddenly one day, the *terra* isn't *firma,* the ground no longer solid but wracked by convulsions. Where then do we turn? What then do we do?

There are two ways to know an earthquake: in the mind or in the bones. In the mind, you can know a quake by reading or hearing about it or visiting the damage afterquake, imagining what it took to produce all the havoc and death. It was in this way I knew the most ferocious quake ever to strike North America, the second greatest by that time ever measured by a seismograph anywhere on earth. A quake that savaged the city of Anchorage, Alaska.

Ironic and chilling it was for Christians that it came on Good Friday, that day for observing the moment of Jesus' death when Matthew's gospel reports "the earth shook and the rocks split." In Alaska rocks didn't just split. In what was classified as a "mega thrust earthquake, the fiercest of all, whole tectonic plates shifted, one plate subducted by another. The earth more than shook, it continued shaking for *three minutes!* It recorded as high as 9.2. Living close to CalTech, seismograph capital of America, we understood that the Richter scale is logarithmic so the difference between, say, an 8.2 and that 9.2 is approximately thirty-fold. The 9.2 thirty times more powerful and likely destructive. And, indeed, when things could be sorted out and tolls tallied, 143 people had been killed; tsunamis and landslides generated; in the city, buildings collapsed and much of the city's infrastructure turned to twisted trash; two hundred miles to the southeast, around Kodiak, the land had been jacked up by some thirty feet while miles from there, around Turnagain Arm land was depressed by eight feet. For a reporter it was one of those assignments that challenges the vocabulary as well as the composure. Sometimes, when showing such horrific scenes, the best narration is silence.

Not as powerful in Richter terms but far more destructive in the relative terms of people and city was another earthquake I got to a day late in Managua, Nicaragua. Late because the airport was shut down immediately upon the quake which killed some ten thousand people and destroyed, it was figured, 90 percent of that capital city. How poignant the scene the next day to visit the American embassy, its building destroyed, staff doing their work out on the grounds, offices hastily set up under trees, desks on the lawn, an office clock nailed to a tree trunk and, propped up proudly on a box marked "Reception," the official seal of the United States of America. Building gone; embassy trying to make it business as usual,

I said there are two ways to know an earthquake: in the mind or in the bones. Traveling to cover the after-effects may put it vividly in your mind but ultimately, only by being there, going through it, will you truly feel the quake, live it deep in inside, know it in your bones.

Our first impression is wrong, so wrong! We think it's Neska, our hundred-twenty pound Great Pyrenees doing what she often does around daybreak, wake us up by leaping up onto the bed – the *water bed!* (We were living in California, you know.) "Surf's up," we joke when she does that. And that's what we say now. Until we look out the bedroom window and see that surf is also up in the swimming pool out there, sloshing out of its containment, splashing across the pool deck. With instant realization, Mary Jo is out of bed dashing toward the kids' room, the earthquake bouncing her off the hallway walls like a pinball careening crazily with me right behind her, reaching the kids room where one of them, unfazed, is still asleep.

Seismologists will claim later that the quake lasted only twelve seconds. I won't believe them. I know it lasts long enough to embed itself forever in my memory. It, and its aftershocks yet to come. The thing about an aftershock is that you are never sure it *is*. An *after*shock, I mean. It could be that what you thought was the main quake a while ago was itself only a *fore*shock. The real quake may be still to come and it will be bigger, perhaps monstrously bigger. It will start the same as an aftershock but then keep growing in magnitude, intensity, terror. You won't know. Every time shaking begins you will hope it will be only an aftershock, stopping quickly and not causing more damage.

As for damage, of course, there are two kinds. One is the structural, – damage to buildings, roads, freeway bridges. In this quake much of that occurred around the epicenter of Sylmar, especially around several hospitals there. 64 people were counted dead from the quake, measured at a 6.6 magnitude.

The other kind of damage an earthquake does is just as real but not as apparent. It won't show on TV or appear in front-page photographs. It is the psychic damage, the nervous trauma and sense of dislocation and perpetual mistrust. Again, if you can't trust the earth . . .

When a quake shakes buildings, they may weaken and crumble. When it shakes people, same results. The mind's self-defense against trauma can be numbness. After an earthquake, you'll find some sensible people behaving insensibly. It happens in wartime, it happens in earthquakes. A poignant example happens in a second quake my wife and I suffer years later. By now we no longer live in L.A. but are back for an ill-timed visit, come to attend one of those show business awards programs and ensconced in the expense account luxury of The Peninsula, one of L.A.'s finest. (Although I never understand the need for the sign prominently displayed by the six-by-six foot spa pool outside our room. Maximum depth: Probably three feet. And the sign: *No Diving.*)

This quake explodes us awake at 4:31 a.m.. We recognize it instantly. And almost instantly, I have tossed on jeans and a T-shirt and am heading toward the lobby while Jo stays behind to attempt a phone call to alert family we're okay. She'll wait for me to return to the room.

In the lobby, first things I notice are the several sturdy marble pedestals, surmounted by heavy marble statuary and what strikes me is that they are not where they were last night. I can tell by the marks on the marble floor. Each of those pedestals has migrated a couple of feet across the floor. Erect but misplaced. Already gathering around the lobby are many people I recognize from last night's festivities.

Some are A&E colleagues, some the celebrity winners, losers or pre-
senters. Most, dressed just as I am, whatever they hastily put their
hands on. T-shirts, pajamas; here's the beautiful Australian fashion
model Elle MacPherson unfashionably attired in baggy grey sweats,
hair stringing. Ah, but look over there, standing by the front desk, a
debonair fellow neatly turned out in well-pressed grey slacks, navy
blazer, open-throated dress shirt with foulard ascot. I walk over to
Tony Bennett and say, "Tony, looks like you even sleep dapper." We
talk for a moment.

By now, most of the sleep-eyed stragglers have moved out the
front doors to stand under the great portico. Cabbies are gathered
out there, one with his car door open and his radio streaming the
news we're all eager to hear.

I am not eager enough to hear it, however, to stand out under that
portico which I can tell, even through the dim light of approaching
dawn, is a lovely but precarious canopy of leaded glass. Glass overhead and tremors still possible?

I return to our room, gather up our things and as we leave the
room, prop the door open because the door locks are electrically
powered and the power is out. In the lobby we mill about with the
other people gathered there some of whom, like Ms. MacPherson,
tried to return to their rooms only to find they can't get in. (In her
case, there are many gallant chaps quick to offer use of their rooms
should she wish. She doesn't.)

Tony Bennett has been joined by his conductor and they take the
opportunity to talk to me about a show idea they have that A&E might
be interested in. I pull one of the network execs into the chat and
hear their pitch which, many months later, will indeed make the air
on A&E, a series of musicals in which the audience phones in requests
and Tony – who knows about every song ever written – immediately
performs. Thus is show business business done in the quavering moments post-earthquake in the powerless lobby of the Peninsula Hotel.

By now it's six or so and the news from the taxicab radio details
extensive areas of damage, destruction, bridges down, roads closed,

airport shut down until at least ten o'clock while officials assess runway damage if any. Our goal, Jo and I decide, is to get out of here as
soon as possible, meaning first out of this hotel and then out of this
city. A couple of friends are with us. One has a cell phone still functioning so he gets on to the New York office and tells them to arrange
flights for Jo and me to Tampa, themselves back to New York. We persuade one of the cabbies to chance it and get us, if he can, to LAX.
The next 45 minutes are instructive as to what roads we thought were
still open that are not. And how to most cautiously approach an underpass, fearful that the road crossing above might be weakened and
might just take the moment of our passing to collapse on top of us. So
the driver stops just short of each underpass, then, as fast as he can
guns it till we're safely on the other side. Then, with a grateful sigh,
resumes careful speed as we snake our way through the city, always
in the general direction of the airport. By the time we finally arrive
we've had return calls on the cell and so head to the American terminal where we read the taxi's meter, double it and add a generous tip
beyond, thanking the driver for his courage and perspicacity.

It is still a few hours before the airport is declared open and we
are permitted to board and slowly the aircraft starts moving, taxiing,
then turning onto the runway, exercising the engines which sound
good to me, sound really good, and the plane surges forward, rolling
down the runway faster, faster and then lifts off the tarmac buoyed by
the sudden, spontaneous cheering and applause of 256 released and
relieved passengers. At that moment, I flash on a singular realization.
This is the first time I have ever been on a plane where I knew exactly
what time each my fellow passengers got up that morning. 4:31 a.m.

I was talking about some of the more subtle, psychic damages an
earthquake can do to people, disrupting normal thought patterns,
numbing sense and senses. One example, and I'm not picking on
my wife but hers at this moment post-quake is an example I know.
To begin with, all the frightening layers of stress have finally been
cleared. The senses can relax as do body and mind. And that's when
one is vulnerable to dissociative phenomena. There is a class of drugs

called dissociative. *Dissociatives are a class of hallucinogen, which distort perceptions of sight and sound and produce feelings of detachment - dissociation - from the environment and self. This is done through reducing or blocking signals to the conscious mind from other parts of the brain.*

A movie comes on. We're all given free headsets, the airline crew's way of acknowledging what we have all been through – as, of course, have they. Jo and I put on our earphones and start watching the film. I would never, in future tellings of the tale, remember what the film was we saw that day. It's not important. But it lasts a couple of hours as we wing our way happily across the land, headed home. Jo seems content throughout the flight but the toll the quake and stress have taken on her are revealed as the movie ends.

"Pretty good," I offer. "You like it?"

"Very unusual," she says. "Interesting technique. Never seen a movie like that."

"Like what? What do you mean?"

"I mean a whole movie with no dialog, no spoken words. Just music. The music fit. It was powerful in some places. The whole film was fascinating, unique."

I look over at her armrest and at mine. My audio control is set to channel two on which I listened to the movie soundtrack, dialog and all for two hours. Hers is set to channel six. Classical music. She wasn't aware. *Dissociation.* The earthquake's one last slam at her sensitive self.

At the top of this chapter, I said my vote for the #1 meanest act of nature went to the earthquake. But I think I need to think again. There is another phenomenon that in itself is a dreadful compounding of nature's meanest. As it rarely affects the continental United States, it is usually ignored in a catalog of cataclysms. It shouldn't be.

Whenever I think of it, I think of Harry Truman. In fact, I think of *two* Harry Trumans. I knew them only posthumously but that never dimmed in my mind the specialness of each. These two were heroes quintessential.

As I think of two Harry Trumans, I think as well of two Washingtons in which those namesakes most notably lived. Hardly more dissimilar could two places in this nation be than the disparate Washingtons – State and District. Fir forests and dark lakes swaddled in softening quilts of fog or snow versus marble monuments attacked by smog from without and more devious pollutants within.

Washington D.C., the nation's capital, constantly twitching with the high voltage sparkings of politics. Washington state, calm in its own stately rhythms.

They are different, those two, but there are likenesses. Each Washington is a place people seek, one for power, one for peace. Places that are peopled by those who haven't just happened by but have come or loyally remained on purpose are the most engaging.

So celebrate the Washingtons but consider then the Harry Trumans, men of Independence and Spirit.

First, Independence. That city in Missouri was home to the failed haberdasher who with nothing else going for him went into politics. Politics took him to Washington, D.C., where, in 1945 he surprisingly found himself President of the United States. Those were not easy times nor were the decisions he had to make in immediate years.

The bomb. Use it or not? How many lives would two atomic bombs dropped in Japan destroy? How many lives would a foreshortened war save? How to decide? Not by reading polls. That's not how Harry Truman decided things. Nor did he make decisions without consulting his own faith, his inner voice. In ways, he was a simple man and not ashamed of his simplicity. Many in politics and public life thought him a buffoon, one of our weaker presidents. Voters thought differently and shocked republicans and the Chicago Tribune by electing him to his own term beginning in 1948.

He was honest. That's what folks thought and it bespoke the sad searching for honesty in so much of our populace in a time of rampant dissembling. By the time of his death, many opinions had softened. If he was countryfied and simple, so were a lot of us. He had dealt with terrible times and got us through them. When our nation needed toughness, he was tough! When later, war over, we sought reconciliation, how this plain-speaking fellow in the baggy grey suits had reconciled! Eulogies were appropriate.

I sat on a light pole. It had a platform surmounting it to afford a view over the fence and into the grounds of the Truman Library in Independence where the funeral services were held. Our platform had been long planned but hastily erected when finally the time had come. I shared the perch with Robert McCormick, NBC's Grand Old Master of Washington. He had been the network's principal reporter of D.C. for decades, covering every president since Roosevelt. He'd been pals with Truman back in that day when reporters could still be pals with presidents. To give you an idea what television was like in those days, Bob's early television reports presumably from the White House or Capitol showed him standing there, the building behind him while he did his piece. So it seemed. In fact, he was in a studio standing there in his trench coat in front of a rear projection screen on which a glass slide of the Capitol or White House as appropriate was displayed. It went well until the evening as he was broadcasting live and heard a sharp cracking sound and turned to see the U.S. Capitol had just been split asunder from top to bottom. Broken slide. Turning back to camera, without a further word Bob read the rest of his piece and tossed it back to John Cameron Swayze in New York. He was cool before we called people that.

Now he – and I – were not just cool but very cold up on our perch reporting the funeral of the man America didn't think it liked until it realized it did.

The "S" in his name meant nothing. Harry S Truman, at a crucial time in his nation's life, meant America.

What, though, to be said about Harry $\underline{R}$. Truman? As S was the man of Independence, R was the man of Spirit, a spirit which seemed for a bright instant in a dark time to be unquenchable. This was in the *other* Washington. Just five years after Americans were singing about S, they were talking about R.

Spirit was a little mountain resort town in southwestern Washington, a hundred miles from Seattle. There was a lodge by a lake in the deep woods beneath a massive mountain, an idyllic get-away from all. Except from nature. Actually people went there to plant themselves more intimately within nature if only for a week or so. The man who ran the lodge – Harry R. Truman – had planted himself there for a lifetime. Now 86, he meant to die there, though he didn't expect it to be quite as soon or quite the way nature had in mind. As Harry S had been the right man in the right time and place, Harry R would be eulogized as the right man in precisely the wrong place and wrong time.

The mountain overshadowing Spirit Lake and Truman's lodge was Mount St. Helen's. Today, we know that name as a synonym for the unequalled ferocity of nature, unleashed. Never before nor since in this country has such force been exhibited as in the eruption of that volcano. Inactive for more than a hundred years, it surprised people when it first began to tremble in what became more frequent and more powerful earthquakes over several months. Though facing considerable opposition, scientists managed to persuade governments to close everything in the area around the volcano. Including Harry Truman's Lodge. They could not, however, convince him to leave. He had run the lodge for over half a century and, he said, it was his life.

A life he lost on May 18th when Mt. St. Helen's finally blew. The enormity of the pyroclastic eruptions and towering ash cloud reached miles into the sky and spread debris and ash for many, many miles across the countryside can, to this day, barely be quantified, hardly imagined. Of the stubborn Mr. Truman, friends figured that had he evacuated and then seen what happened to his mountain and his lake and his lodge, that would have killed him anyhow.

Neither before nor since in the lower '48 had there been such natural destruction. Now, these decades later, it still shows. It benumbs. I spent days wandering the area shaking my head. From a distance one may not recognize Mt. St. Helen's as a stunted mountain. Won't find Spirit Lake; it's gone. But you will find trees. Hundreds of thousands of trees. Flat. Anywhere 20 miles from the blast trees were felled – stripped of branches, leaves, bark, flattened on the ground as though a giant were ready to begin a fiendish game of pickup sticks. That's how it struck me, mile upon mile. I came to a lake, far below my road. Looking down upon it, I puzzled at something strange. The entire end of the lake, maybe a third of its surface, was different. No sun sparkled off the water at that end. It took binoculars to realize that that entire end of the lake was clotted with logs, fallen trees blasted into the lake and still clogging this much of it's surface. Further removed from the volcano's epicenter, I found forests mostly standing but also stripped, of branch, leaf and hope. In these are forlorn forests one is forced to remember what he cannot forget.

Jackstraws

So many years ago it was,
The day the mountain blew
Forces primeval
Forces evil
Exploding in fiery, liquid rock
Blast furnace winds raging
Three hundred miles an hour
(Hurricane times two)
Ripping and stripping
Such that for miles and miles around
Forests mature were felled and strewn
Stripped to whips
Scattered about like pickup sticks
With no one left to pick them up

Today those barren poles and tumbled jackstraws
Pose a question unanswerable
God made the forest
God made the mount
God made us to witness
How one took the life of the other
Why?
That, God does not explain
It remains Mt. St. Helen's haunting enigma.

ROADSIDE

I tremble. I hurt. Have to pull off, can't look back. I didn't mean it to happen, I didn't. But it happened. And, in haunted recall, it still happens.

It's a narrow country road. I'm going one way, a car is coming from the other direction when across my vision bursts a blur jerking this way and that as squirrels do when panicked. I can't veer and I can't stop. It misses the car coming toward me and disappears under my car, dashes under mine and I pray it won't happen but it does and I hear the thump. I have killed it. I have destroyed that little spirit. I hear the thump, the awful thump of the small body being crushed beneath one of my wheels. *Thump-crunch!* It is over.

As quickly as I get a chance, I pull to the side of the road. Not to look back. I can't look back. I sit here. I hurt and I shake and I want to cry but cleansing tears won't come. Can there be no cleansing?

Calm! Summon reason. An eastern brown squirrel, the species is classified. (Taxonomy objectifies the creature; that should make this easier.) The species is common; not an endangered species or even threatened. That's comforting. Isn't it? The animal breeds in winter months. These are winter months. Its principal predators, books confirm are humans.

Me.

But it's only an animal, screams a voice inside, trying to restore my composure. *It's a rodent, that's all it is.*

Was.

Hesitantly, I pull my car back onto the road, not shaking now though still pained. I go only a hundred yards when something else flashes across my vision and I start. No! Something astonishingly blue swoops and darts across right to left. Blue so vivid it hurts. It is another creature of God, an eastern bluebird. Flying free. Alive. (Come to cleanse?)

Then, another couple hundred yards along, as though another piece of solace and consolation, comes flashing a new dart of color, this one stunningly bright, red aflame, swooping right to left across the road, a male cardinal.

Given these two flashing reminders of God's priceless gift of life I should begin to feel better now, shouldn't I?

Shouldn't I?

It's months later that I experience a moment of at least imagined balance. It is not the same road but could be. Again narrow, coiled around these Georgia hills, clinging to them. This road is dirt and as I round a bend I am struck by a sight I have tried so long to forget. In the road lies the carcass of a squirrel. Hunched over it, feeding on it, a black vulture. Some other driver has run the squirrel down, killing it with either remorse or disregard – probably the latter – and the bird now is doing its job, nature's assignment, cleaning up carrion. The cycle in completion. Except again, I have interfered. The vulture flies off, for now at least, its meal denied.

BISON, BISON, BISON

I shouldn't have said it out loud. I was talking to myself; there was no need to blow speak-breath into the air to fog and freeze on my goggles. It was hard enough jouncing up the rutted mountain track at twenty miles an hour. I didn't need to shout to my shivering self over the blatting of the engine, but I felt such distress that I hollered loud enough to hear myself hollering. I yelled: *I cannot remember ever being so cold!*

A gelid hell it was, not prickling or stinging cold, beyond those, far beyond those. Fingers, toes, and cheeks do not prickle or sting when fingers, toes, and cheeks cannot feel, when sharp sensation has escaped, supplanted by throbbing ache. I had known cold before, other times, other places, but had it ever been this bad? Could anyplace ever have been this bad?

Of course it could; of course it had. Human nature always wants our immediate situation to be singular and superlative. The highest, the fastest, the greatest, even *the coldest*. We are people who thrive on *-ests*.

But, in fact, I *had* been that cold before. Even colder by thermometer measurement in other times, other places. Up on the North Slope of Alaska; in Barrow, northernmost town in our nation; along Prudhoe Bay among the oil rigs spread across the tundra – those I had traveled in younger years. And Fairbanks. A two week tour in

Fairbanks, Alaska where for most of the time I never found temperatures much above that point of tortured conjunction where Celsius
meets Fahrenheit. People living in that area are familiar with trans-
posing one scale to the other. The point where they meet can be
calculated by using formulae (9/5 or 5/9 plus 32 or minus 32 ... or
something.) Or, by simple mathematical trial and error as I did one
night in a frigid Alaskan bar where the shock of the night came when
my TV cameraman, producer and I heard a beefy, flanneled bear of
a woman bellying the bar demanding "Everclear, vodka back" and we
got thinking that whatever this Everclear was, if you used vodka as
a chaser, Everclear must be *something* and we had to try it. (We were
men determined to prove we were *men*!) The bartender, demonstrat-
ing, poured a dab of Everclear onto a saucer and lit it. It burned
with a pure blue flame! We ordered shots, sampled cautiously, then
slugged them down and got back to our puzzle. *Let's see, If Fahrenheit
is, let's try minus forty, then Centigrade would be... Oh, heck, let's get some
more Everclear. Fella? Thanks, slug, Phewww! Where were we? Okay, say
Fahrengrade is minus forty then Centiheit must be* ... Eureka!. Minus 40
degrees was the 180 proof solution.

Actually, in Fairbanks those nights it was even colder than that.
Minus 55F, I remember hearing. *Minus 55!* That kind of cold impressed. You quickly ran out of adjectives. The *knifing, slicing* genre
of words were left behind. "Bone-chilling," apart from being clichéd
was inadequate. That kind of cold didn't just chill it did far more
than that. And not only to bone, it worked into the very marrow.
People who live in places like that are well aware of the dangers, how
few minutes of exposure skin can endure before turning white and
prickly then numb and dying.

That does something to people, and to everything that hasn't already lost its life. Fairbanks streets looked like a herpetologist's nightmare, snake skins strewn everywhere, lifeless victims of too many days
and too many nights of fatal freeze. *Snake skins?* In Fairbanks? In cold
so cold has the mind, itself, frozen, sharp sensations escaped, supplanted by dull throbbing nonsense? But no, those lifeless snakes,

carrion strewn across the hardened snow that is winter's pavement here, have no heads and have no tails – fan belts never do. Fan belts, timing belts, the rest.

The power of extreme cold is cumulative so that after relentless days and nights, almost all oscillations of warmth vanish from particles of matter. In that kind of cold, walls of a house no longer warm but drain warmth away. Flesh unprotected is frostbitten in seconds. Gas in fluorescent lights freezes if lights are turned off. That, I thought in black letter boldface, is **cold**!

I wouldn't let myself think of Fairbanks that day getting crotch-pounded astride the muscle machine I had been assigned to ascend the frigid flanks of Two Peaks mountain in Idaho. I wouldn't entertain any suggestion that this was not in fact the fiercest freeze I had ever endured. I had donned layers – many layers – of high-tech winter underwear and even the old low-tech pair of cashmere long johns I had picked up ages before in the far east. I wore a heavy flannel shirt under an expedition-weight down parka with faux-fur collar and downfilled hood which was pulled over a tightly knit wool skull cap. All that. And still . . .

I cannot remember ever being so cold!

Forty below was the chatter – teeth-chattering chatter? – around the town of West Yellowstone, Montana that January morning. It was reported that a gash of extreme freeze had knifed its way over the park bringing these unusual conditions. The park was closed on that morning, rangers and maintenance men not yet able to get out and clear the ice-strewn trails. The sun was out but you sensed it didn't want to be. If its job was to warm the earth, that day, in that place, it knew it had no chance.

With Yellowstone temporarily closed, we decided to play somewhere else, outside the park, heading our little caravan of foolhardy (more the first syllable than the second) photographers on snowmobiles across the state border into Idaho to jerk and jolt our roaring way up the rugged flanks of Two Peaks. The ascent would take forty-five minutes. It was a beautiful winterscape, true, the snow-choked streams sparkling trailside, the snow-laden branches drooping to dump their gentle and not unwelcome loads on passing heads, and once or twice a sudden flash of feathers across the monochrome scene. It was beautiful (though I would never truly appreciate that until reviewing the pictures back in a warm room hours later.) The bones of the human frame – the middle-aged human frame – are not as well cushioned as one being hurled about by a raging snowmobile might wish. So the double joy of finally reaching our destination, the top of Two Peaks, and dismounting was part physical relief for aching body and part astonishment at the surreality we found. How to describe the scene?

The top of the mountain was a shallow bowl several hundred yards in diameter which appeared to have been transformed into a most unusual art museum, the current show being a display of astonishing marble sculpture. There were large and imposing pieces filling the gallery – giant statuary of heroic proportions lining the rim of the bowl, while, scattered about as though haphazardly but likely well planned by the curator, were smaller abstract whimsies remindful of Picasso or Miro, even a couple of pieces so gaunt as to suggest Giacometti. There were massive Michelangelos at least twice the size of his *David*, relaxed Rodins, and some works so peculiar they must have been Dali or Leger. What all of them had in common was that all of them were white. Pure, clean, sparkling white as though their marble had been feverishly polished for this magnificent *vernissage* at which we were the honored guests, VIP's in padding, helmets and mitts.

I could put it another way. Think of a photographer coming upon that mountaintop scene. To him – especially if numbed and suffering brain-freeze from the ride up – it looked as though he took a photograph of a stunning landscape scene, tall dark trees ringing the plateau, the bowl of the plateau filled with wind-twisted trees, gnarled bushes and sprigs in their many dark shades of green, except that the photographer is not looking at the print of the picture, he is viewing the negative. Everything appears in reverse polarity, blacks white, whites black. Surreal. And then, even as his mind is still twisting around that puzzle of ice-white sculptures and reverse-polarity photographs, he must once more mount his glacial steed and torturously convulse back down the mountain. Screaming all the way.

> **I can't remember ever being so cold!**
> *You can't? Try. Try to remember your days*
> *Of discomfort, of danger; the terrible times of trial*
> *When chilling specters of peril precluded a smile,*
> *When you felt yourself frigid with fear like the icy displays*
> *On that Idaho mount. Try. These are tales to be told*
>
> *At long-after huddles when yarns of courage are spun*
> *And you spin your own, and even embroider the tale*
> *Of flash-frozen mummies on wind-torn hill and you*
> *Locked in that gelid hell, no way to subdue*
> *Only to be subdued – so you regale*
> *Listeners more but with that, you are done*
>
> *Your time in gelid hell is a tale to be told*
> *But also a test. You may shy from tests but shouldn't*
> *You need them in order to grow. You cannot count*
> *Yourself complete until you've climbed your mount*
> *That frozen, windy peak you thought you couldn't*
> *And still can't remember ever being so cold*
>
> *You suffered but you also learned to cope*
> *With suffering and grow through times of stress*
> *As Paul in Romans wrote his adherents*
> *Suffering produces perseverance*
> *Perseverance, character, and yes*
> *Character, in turn, produces hope*

The next day was no warmer but some of the park's trails had been cleared so our entourage, again well-layered and bundled, re-mounted our machines and headed out into the Yellowstone of geysers and bison. The former we would have to go to; the latter we would find in abundance along our way. Along *their* way I should say for, in winter, Yellowstone's trails and roads are dedicated to bison, largest land mammals in America. They have first rights, because they have the greatest need to conserve their precious energy in this challenging climate. So rather then make the ponderous animals plow through deep snow banks they are able to walk the cleared roads while approaching snowmobiles, snow-cats and snowcoaches are required to pull off and stop to let the animals pass.

Which, for explorers with cameras, is ideal. Here come five animals in a line, a lumbering bison procession. Hastily, I set up in a dip at the side of the road, lower than the level of the bison as they move silently across the field of snow before me. Snow below, snow on the hillside beyond, yield a silhouetted, monochrome parade. .

At length, the bison highway leads us to the first of Yellowstone's renowned geysers, their steamy breaths teasing us with a warmth we will not know this day. There are geysers other places but none as famed as those in Yellowstone. Most of all, Old Faithful. Photographed so many times by tourist cameras snap-shooting for Facebook friends that I am disinclined to work here. Let this be one of the photographer's undocumented moments, a time not to picture nature but to ingest it, absorb it, bringing home not just another oft-replicated postcard but a singular and altogether original memory. Mental pictures are always in focus and perfectly exposed.

On we go. Back on the snowmobiles, jolting and jouncing toward – what? We know not. Photography's best opportunities, like life's, are not advertised or expected. God provides. (And should I say that to my companions on this trip I would be mocked or politely ignored.)

We make a few stops to shoot mist clouds over warm geyser pools, ethereal dream scenes. Then we come to a river, and here we witness how hard winter can be for the bison population of Yellowstone. We see it in one animal, alone, no others around. He is standing at the bank of a frozen river, all shaggy and snow-clothed, steam-breath pumping from the nostrils of his massive head. He is hoping to eat, to find some slight nourishment on this impossible day the likes of which he knows too well. From a small bridge, I am looking down at him without *looking down on him*. There is no demeaning this great beast. There is astonishment that he and his kin persist and survive. What he is doing at the moment seems a measure of futility his wintertime life lays on him each day. Simply to find sustenance to carry him, heat him and keep him alive. At the moment his broad head is nose down in the show, digging, burrowing, foraging. Is there anything down there on which to feed? Any green plants surviving under the snow? Must be something. Has to be *something!* He will spend all day trying. It is his life in balance.

I like to think it is that same animal that I see six months later on the other side of the park. It isn't no doubt, but I like to think. He stands now regally, proudly atop a hill as I drive the road below. Beyond him are peaks of the Tetons but seen only dimly, interposing mists veiling them.

I stop the car, take out my camera and step out slowly, cautiously. He looks straight at me. I appreciate the truth that, monumental and iconic as they appear, bison can be dangerous. I will not push him. But I fix my eyes on him and my mind on him as well. For me, the moment is a passing but transcendental encounter.

> *The original American,*
> *Proud pretender of the plains;*
> *Once he ranged in myriads*
> *Of which but memory remains*

Today, to guarantee all eyes,
All minds, all focus be on him
The over-towering mountains deign
To shroud themselves behind a scrim

That he alone, in ragged robe,
Shakespearean, commands the stage,
Soliloquizing in the mist,
This icon of another age.

Buffalo, some people say
Who haven't checked the formal list.
For "Bison bison bison" decreed
A stammering taxonomist

A treble name to comprehend
This ponderous ton of antiquity
Yielder of meat, provider of warmth,
And occasional iniquity.

This greatest beast is more to be feared
By man than wolf or cat or bear
And yet, and yet, something happens that day.
I think it happens. Let me share:

I step from behind the camera and climb
The grass of his hill, an exercise
That brings me gazing into his gaze,
Those knowing orbs, those ancient eyes.

Grasping his horns I slowly lower
My forehead to his; he does not stir.
Neither of us is surprised as it happens,
Cool skin cleaving to his warm fur.

The steam of his breathing moistens my face
I inhale the damp and close my eyes
Close my eyes but still can see,
Though not as before, and I realize

No longer am I without, gazing in,
But somehow I am within seeing out,
Seeing as he sees. How can that be?
I don't understand but do not doubt.

I sense in my sinews a confounding truth
That a transformation has begun:
I am become he, looking down, seeing me:
And we are kin, and we are one.

I raise my gaze to a milky sky
That has no shape or form or face
And yet I know it, know that from it
Somehow I feel comfort. Place

Me on my hill or in a meadow,
Or out across the plain and I
Will always be connected to
The power of that milky sky.

It gives me freedom, finds me grass,
Gives me all I know as real.
I guess it even provides this very
Curious feeling that I feel.

But wait. No longer cool skin against my fur
That's not what I'm feeling now.
I'm feeling – How strange, and yet how familiar! –
I'm feeling warm fur beneath my brow.

Releasing the horns, I raise my head
And there again are those ancient eyes.
Ponderous One and ponderer,
Each the other in disguise.

Or am I daft? Was it all chimera?
Can transmigration ever be?
Still, I stick to my story. After all, a group
Of us bison is called an Obstinacy

HONKERS, 'SHINE AND A MILLION BIRDS

T
he stream does not belong to us. Oh, there is a piece of paper that says our land extends halfway across to where our cross-creek neighbor's land begins. A paper says that. I say the stream does not belong to me, nor I to it. It's just that when we built our mountain house, we chose to build beside it. Even for me, a non-angler, there is allure to a place on a north Georgia trout stream.

Strategically, then, we sited the house along that stretch of the stream where our property would be bracketed on two corners by tumbling rapids – not ferocious falls, rapids class three or four, but constantly burbling water. Even in summer with its interposing leaf-drapes when we can't see the rapids, we are soothed by their aural massage.

A greater joy, of course, is to sit down at the edge of the stream and watch the waters pass, observing as well those who pass with it. There are the silent passersby, the fish themselves. Some of those go by. Some just swim around without leaving, the comfortable backwater pools their home. Upstream a couple hundred yards or so is a relic remindful that fish have been coursing Mountaintown Creek since long before it had that name. Native people fished here for many scores if not centuries past. At one point, they used rocks to construct a weir across the stream's flow to partially dam the waters and raise their levels creating something of a pond. Likely they strung stakes and nets then to gather basking trout for harvest. It is the nature of the fish today that some of them still pass along the watercourse while many find favorable refuges in backwater pools, still waters in which they settle and make their homes, letting their unwary food come to them. A trout fishing teacher told us that if we wished we could have a reliable source of browns or rainbows for pan-fried breakfasts as often as we wished if we would simply begin feeding them. Scatter trout food (there *is* such a thing?) across the still pools and backwaters where they hang out and they would be quite accommodating and stick around, reproducing breakfast after breakfast for us. Two problems. I don't fish. Mary Jo fishes but doesn't gut and clean. Plus which, for breakfast I prefer peanut butter toast and fruit. And then there's this: Wouldn't feeding the fish to keep them around solely so you could catch and eat them be on the scale of human imposition, even cruelty, as baiting bear or spreading corn around your deer stand? Or, for that matter, luring pintails with duck calls? Yes, subsistence hunting is different but of "sport" hunting I am neither participant nor fan.

Christmas goose? Couldn't. In my life (sheltered, some may deem it to be) wild birds provide more nourishment as they are – wild!

What a lifting joy to hear announced by gravelly squawks the approach of a skein of honkers using the flight path the stream has cleared through woods on either side. Magnificent birds, these Canada geese. Magnificent to see and warming just to know they are with us, if only for a passing moment.

As so often with wildlife, it's a one-way love. Intent on their journey, why should they take note of the creature squatting on the hillside up from the bank of the creek? What sort of creature might it be? How should they know or care? That creature does not seem to threaten them. I hold no shotgun, have no shotgun, never have, never will. I'd like the geese to know that, to be assured that I can be trusted. But, on the other hand, if they learned to trust me, gained confidence to take me for granted, who might get them downstream?

Better for them to maintain their species' inbred wariness; it serves them well.

It is one thing to spy a raft of honkers at rest on a pond, floating, silent. One thing to watch them hungrily poking among grasses pondside. One thing to watch them then tuck heads beneath wings to doze. All those are treasured moments but to watch them winging and wending above our stream uplifts and inspirits.

It's wonderful how the sight and sound of birds can do that. Wonderful how God, through those avian instruments, does that.

It might be but a single bird. How long I can sit transfixed by the invisible wings on the tiny thing hovering before me – the feisty but delicate, aggressive while appearing so harmless — ruby-throated hummingbird. It's one thing to read the stats: weight, less than a nickel; length, 3 inches; the bird cannot walk, it's legs too short and set too far back; wing speed, 55 strokes *a second*; speed, 30 mph; meaning, when one of them migrates from, say North Georgia each year to wintering grounds in Central America, part of that trek will be a nonstop flight crossing the Gulf of Mexico, a distance of more than ten million times the bird's own length. For me to make a trek comparable to my own body length I'd be traveling almost half way around the world. The hummer makes his Gulf crossing in 17 hours. Mine would take appreciably longer even if I hitched commercial flights. During the hummingbird's crossing, his wings will beat three-and-a-third million times. Heck, at rest, his pulse is twelve hundred. He breathes 250 times a minute. The little fellow is a preposterous creation!

And that's just the statistical bird. While the numbers boggle, what entrances and excites me is the ruby-throat's astonishing beauty. At first, I see no ruby throat. Looks black. There is no red coloration to the miniature feathers of the hummer's throat. Ah, but there is an almost magical iridescence that with light flashes brilliant ruby rays directly at me, as though the color were emanating directly from the throat, not being brightly reflected by it.

I spy him perching on a small twig halfway up the trunk of a sour-wood. He has our sugar-water feeder staked out as *his own*. Between frequent visits, (he has to eat half his body weight in sugar every day, dining an average a half-dozen times an hour) he keeps an eye out from his twig to ensure no intruder tries to muscle in on his stash. If one tries – *ZOOM!* – down dives the jealous one to shoo the interloper away. An aerial battle ensues, chasing, fleeing, then changing roles as fleer becomes chaser and round and round and up and down they whiz and surge, until one escapes and the other (Original Bossbird?) is back on the lookout twig and I am left wondering if aerial battles among Top Guns pilots of fighter planes, instead of being called "dogfights," mightn't more aptly be spoken of as "Hummer fights." So I wonder, but not for long for as soon as twig-bird swoops down to sip from the feeder again, here comes the other pilot to drive this one away. Hard to know for whom to root. So I sit back, not trying to understand, just enjoying the show put on by a couple of God's most astounding creations.

If two birds can thrill like that, what might happen with a million?

A million birds at one sight! In front of me, on either side, behind me, flashing overhead, swirling all around, shuttering the sunrise as they fly by blinding tens of thousands.

It's an early November morning in Northern California, hard against the Oregon border. Tule Lake, this trackless spread of soil and wetlands is called, a federal wildlife refuge that every year at spring and fall attracts all sort of migratory birds passing through – first the northern pintails, and greater white-fronted geese followed by mallard ducks, American wigeon, green-winged teal, snow, Ross', and Canada geese.. The snows are the most remarkable for their stunning black-and-white patterns, at first tucking away their black wingtips to assume the clean gleam of white all over. Gathering as they like to do with their own kin, they lay a broad, plush carpet of undulating snow across lake and fields. That's how hundreds of thousands of snow geese appear. While at rest. But then . . . .

It isn't right. I wouldn't do it. Many may not know the technique. At a refuge like this, you'll find impatient photographers eager for shots of birds *en masse* taking flight trying to goad them by shouting at them, loudly clapping hands as the birds casually ignore all noises and gesticulations. They stay stubbornly fixed. Photographers must wait until birds, on their own, decide to fly. Or a ranger gets a shovel.

I won't name names. Perhaps he shouldn't have done it for our camera crew. It was a kind accommodation for us if not for the birds. He didn't dig anything except to scoop up dirt at the edge of the lake. "You ready?" he asked us. "Ready" said our cameraman. Wherewith, the ranger whirled the shovelful of loose dirt and gravel up into the air perhaps ten feet, creating a rattling dust cloud bright-lit by morning sun, an alarm which instantly had birds taking flight. So immediate was their reaction that it seemed that half of the geese were airborne before the gravel began clattering down on the waters and shore. By the time the dust cloud had dissipated there was hardly a bird still down.

"How'd ya like that," the ranger asked. "Want me to do it again when they settle?" Before the cameraman could yell yes, cameramen always wanting one more take, I shouted, "No, no thanks, that was great." And the scene, viewed and re-viewed later was indeed a great, thrilling spectacle of downy white birds carpeting the refuge then suddenly bursting into the skies, white and black projectiles scatter-gunned into the air, filling the sky, morning erupted into a frantic, flying crisis. Most of a million creatures wheeling around and above, only a few, off on the perimeter, still at rest, not caught up in the maelstrom. The others, group by group, would slowly settle once more. White carpet calmed, morning right. And I would have a memory ineradicable.

I've wandered, I know, strayed far from a couple of miniature hummingbirds, the thrill of watching those. Far from a parade of honking honkers following the highway of a North Georgia trout stream.

Far from that stream itself and what it *used to mean.*

It helped create a curious part of our nation's history. To think back on that time requires a sense I think of as backward imagining or *Recreativity.*

Wander. Let your mind wander. A mind allowed to wander is a wonder. Discourage not the young from flights of fancy for those flights can raise them to shimmering realms of imagination. It is from imagination that springs all creativity and it is creativity that gives life zest and worth. Even for the older among us fancy flights are useful to return us to places and times we used to know or never did but wish we had. That's *recreativity.*

I take such flights up in the mountains when the air is chilled and stream waters warm and mists begin to rise over the creek. I sit on the hillside fancying, imagining that those are not mists I see this morning but smoke and steam rising many, many mornings ago, the exhalations of a hidden phalanx of copper pot stills up and down this very creek, in this very valley. This was the country for that, you see. Whatever you may have heard – the clichés and caricatures of toothless, tobacco-spittin' 'shiners, shotguns at the ready for pesky revenooers nosin' 'round – whatever you have heard or read or seen in movies or TV and figured was just make-believe, figure again. It happened, it all happened, and here is where. These four counties of north Georgia saw the greatest concentration of corn-liquor moon-shine stills anywhere in the country. And not that long ago. Not long ago at all.

Georgia's former Governor, former Senator and product of the north Georgia mountains, the beloved Zell Miller, told the story in a book recalling ways of mountain life that used to be but by now have mostly disappeared – a book with the charmingly colloquial title: *"Purt Nigh Gone."*

He wrote of ancient origins, not glossing over the church's historic ties to distilled spirits, for centuries Catholic monaster-ies guarding the secrets of distillation, until passing them on to innovative Scots and Irishmen who, to escape new taxes on their whiskeys, immigrated to a new country, bringing with them their equipment and their recipes, arriving mostly in Pennsylvania, then winding their ways down mountain routes into the Carolinas and the Blue Ridge mountains where they began what would be called their "whiskey farming." The resource most available to them was corn and so that's what they used. Corn liquor they began crafting for themselves, their families and a few friends. The crafting was not intended as a business but to make a few coins with which to buy necessities of their simple lives.

The classic still was secluded in hollows and coves along the many creeks and streams in mountain country. And there were a lot of them. Federal agents at the end of the Civil War estimated at least 3,000 stills in the southern mountains, each one turning out as much as 50 gallons of 'shine every day.

By the time of Prohibition (and it started first of all in the state of Georgia), the character of creekside distilling changed. The mountain men had always thought of their making of corn whiskey as a craft, a talent, a skill, as well as a way to make a sustenance living for his family. He did not get rich from this nor think it to be either illegal or immoral. For the most part, he was Christian (likely Presbyterian) and devout.

With Prohibition, however, moonshine did become a business, often run by nascent criminal enterprises. The vehicles used to transport the whiskey through mountains with sketchy roads were juiced up to by ingenious mechanics – an augury of things to come. Down those roads, it was figured, flowed more than a million gallons of illegal whiskey to Atlanta from this corner, our corner, of Georgia. Meanwhile, the skills learned by mountain mechanics in terms of dual manifolds, carburetors and high-compression cylinders were lessons that race car mechanics use yet today. Indeed, there are many reasons to claim that the NASCAR of today rose from the moonshine racers of these Georgia mountains. Dawsonville makes that claim for its town with signs, a NASCAR museum and annual festivities.

Are there insights about God to conclude from tales of long-ago moonshine? It was men of God who originated distilling in their monasteries; other men of God who brought their recipes and stills to our mountains intending them as a craft to support their families. It's interesting that today we reverence the monks and mock the 'shiners.

We are people of God; we are not God.

CAMP MOOSEWOOD

Richard Louv had it right. His book of some years back was titled *Last Child in the Woods.* That was good; a title need not explicate as long as it engages. It was his subtitle, then, that nailed his point: *Saving Our Children from Nature-Deficit Disorder.*

Clever phrase and apt. You've seen it, I've seen it. Anyone who gaily peregrinates through woods, along mountain tracks, across desert, beside river banks, on ocean fronts or lakesides – who imbibes nature as a tonic to refresh heart and soul, can only bemoan that so many younger folk could not care less for nature unless it's displayed on the movie screen where an armored knight gallops across alien plains to slay ferocious, mythical beasts, or in a video game where a combat marine burdened with every weapon of war yet invented or imagined slogs through wicked, foggy woods to attack and destroy other men equally burdened but not as fast on the draw. Those are kids in the woods today, but the wrong woods teaching the wrong lessons.

How has this happened? Parents are not innocent. Grownups had gadgets first. I cannot forget a sorry scene out in the midst of Acadia National Park, out along the rocky coast at a cove where, given accommodating state of tide and direction of wind, waves crash into a small cavern in the rock just below sea-level, exploding the pocket of air and being forced back out in a thunderous roar of sea-spray cannonading thirty or forty feet up in the air. It's a breathtaking spectacle and the site is appropriately named "Thunder Hole."

One day as I was out photographing along that stretch of coast, I watched as an out-of-state van hastily pulled up to a parking spot along Park Loop road, the driver, a man in a hurry, jumped out of the front seat with his video camera to dash down to Thunder Hole, and when the side door of the van also began to open for kids to come along, he yelled at them, "Stay there. Get back in. We can all see it when we get home." And he ran to the shore, shot his video for maybe thirty seconds, got one wave crashing, one shoot of spray and then hurried back to the van to drive on and find what else there was to see along the Loop that the kids could watch on video once they got home. In such a case, don't blame the kids.

Nor in many other cases. Think of all the homeowners associations, condo boards, and community organizations packed with retired business executives (and those who never made it that far up a corporate ladder but this is their chance). Now, bored, they get on a board so they can fill their days between tee times and made-up errands by conjuring up new *Rules* and *Codes* that everyone in their community must obey. No kids serve on these boards so their voices are not heard. Wouldn't matter if they were. Boards are prone to think negative, write rules that deny, exclude, enjoin. Kids are inclined to be positive, pushing limits, rebelling against rules, exploring and adventuring. Know of any forts kids have built in a gated community? What officious adults don't prohibit, they discourage.

Even at places whose dedicated purpose is to attract everyone, including kids, to nature. Go to parks or nature centers today and all too often you will find many – all too many –signs commanding *No Touch* or *Keep Off*. We understand that conservators of such places don't want their grounds trampled, branches broken, flowers picked. Understood. But as far as kids are concerned the over-protectors might just as well surround their sites with electrified razor wire. That would be no more off-putting. Kids learn by touching, appreciate by taking samples, are encouraged by being trusted, discouraged by being repeatedly denied. The point of parks and nature sites should not be to try to kid-proof them. For one thing, it can't be done. For another, it shouldn't. Invite. Don't harp on what kids are not allowed to do; give them places and ways to do it. That is how the kid begins to learn. Nature will heighten a kid's interest and then, if he or she turns to an adult for guidance, the adult's role is not to teach but simply to help the child learn.

I speak from memorable – albeit limited – experience.

Living at Moosewood, just the two of us amid the spangled splash of God's nature, we felt fortunate, to be sure, but also a bit selfish. The question that nagged was not so much *Why are we allowed to have this all for ourselves?* but *Shouldn't we find ways to share the magic of this place?*

One way – Jo's way – was to picture it, share it through her art.

My way was through the thoughts that came to me as I was out and about "cruising snaps" – photographing. If you will forgive the homonym attack I'll say that fixing God's nature in sight incited in-sights and insights resolved into verse.

The Deep Wood
Dappled and dear
Never out of it's mothers sight
A yearling gambols and frisks in the wood
The deep wood

Light chases dark
Blots of shadow, flashes of sun
Dance about the mossy knobs in the wood –
The deep, mottled wood

There is a thrush within
A bird we are blessed to hear but rarely see
Truth told, it is not much to see
But, oh, it is much to hear

As it tootles its liquid flute
Unseen in the wood –
The deep, mottled, melodic wood

Should you one day choose to step through the frame
And into the wood
(And you should;
It is not enough to gaze from without;
You must fairly inhabit the wood
That the wood, evermore, may inhabit you)
Your eyes will gambol along with the fawn,
Dance with the chasing light,
Ears thrill to the liquid fugue of life.
And your soul?
Your soul will calm
In the sanctuary of the deep, mottled, melodic, inhabiting
wood

That was my way. But then Jo and I together developed yet another way. We called it Camp Moosewood. Congress, goaded by the National Park Service, had just passed a law that for the first time set formal boundaries for Acadia National Park and we, the sole residents of Bar Island, were within that boundary. Our cabin, Moosewood, was thus officially designated an in-holding which meant several things. Principally, we had to obey park policies. When the park had relevant policies, that is. Example: We petitioned the park's chief naturalist for permission to place bluebird houses which we would construct on trees around the perimeter of the meadow. It was many weeks before we got a reply: No, we couldn't, we were told, not because it would be contrary to Acadia's policy but because park people realized to their embarrassment that they had not yet written a policy. They didn't have a bluebird policy so we couldn't have bluebirds We were reminded of the cynical rule for dealing with bureaucracies: Smarter to ask forgiveness after than permission before.

Other policies we did have to obey: we couldn't run a business from our place, expand our house by more than 25%, clear paths through the woods or cut down a live tree with a trunk greater than six inches in diameter – none of which we wanted to do. We were permitted (or was it that we forgot to ask?) to salvage a straight pole of driftwood ten feet long from along the shore and haul it awkwardly up to the meadow and along the narrow, natural path created by countless footfalls over numberless summers, maneuvering it clumsily around bends and turns, up the hillside leading to the island's peak, 170 feet above the sea. There, we were not proscribed (since they didn't know) from gathering together a mound of granite chunks and slabs to support the pole onto which we had affixed a small pulley and cleat to complete our makeshift flagpole. This was enough years ago that there was no question what flag we would fly. The stars and stripes were still honored in America and we flew them proudly from the peak, the waving flag easily seen from over in town or from the boats or cruise ships in port. Park Service never complained.

What we could not get away with, naturally, was to open a commercial camping operation on the island so when I say we founded Camp Moosewood, I quickly explain. It wasn't a business, we didn't make money, campers were limited in number and it wasn't a full-time operation (though when a couple of kids were in residence, it seemed to us far more than full time.)

It was not, as so many are, a Camp For Underprivileged Children. On the contrary, we came to call it our Camp for *Overprivileged* Children. Each year for many years, friends of ours from back in our former hometown of Los Angeles had their daughter and any buddy she chose to bring along that year fly across the country and become the only campers for two weeks at Camp Moosewood. Our friends' daughter did this for six or seven years as she approached and entered her teenage time. It was something she and her friends looked forward to and Mary Jo and I found not only challenging but charmingly amusing.

They were *over*privileged back home, perhaps. But camp slowly taught them they were somewhat *under*privileged as well, denied, in their normal lives back home many of the joys they discovered at Camp Moosewood. And what were those? It's a curious list. One of their newfound joys was *doing dishes!* "Our maids would never let us do this," they burbled happily as they swished dinner plates around the foamy water. "Anyhow, we have a machine to wash the dishes. Why don't you?." *Swish, swirl, swish.*

Another joy came on laundry day. We had a machine for that but preferred to hang the wet clothes outside to dry. The girls had never heard of that and jumped into the work eagerly, using wooden clothes pins (also unheard of) to secure sheets, towels and clothing to the line at the edge of the island where the sea breezes would go to work. After which, the great joy of sleeping on those spanking fresh, sea-perfumed sheets that night.

Ah, but not before Lamplight theater. And that righteous ritual could only happen after baths, before prayers.

Each camper, on arrival, had been presented with her own whistle on a lanyard to call if she needed anything. They weren't meant for this, but the girls always seemed to find many things they absolutely had to have while sloshing about, the two of them, in the evening bath. *Whistle, giggles, whistle, laughter.*

While Mary Jo was answering their playful calls I was readying the living room for the next act. Solar-powered electric lights out. A few candles lit around the room and, by my chair, a kerosene lamp fired, and story selected. Poe, it was the first night. *Telltale Heart.* They'd said they wanted scary. And here, freshly scrubbed and with clean jammies, came the girls to gather expectantly around on the floor for the nightly offering in Lamplight Theater.

I gave it my best Karloffian performance, overplaying because they seemed to enjoy that and I certainly did. As evenings went on, however, I began hearing whispers of discontent from my audience. The problem? "Don't you have anything scarier?" Edgar Allen Poe wasn't scary enough for the kids? How kids had changed. I, as a kid, could never bear up through a Poe story. One night I scanned my shelves and found what should be a perfect upgrade. If this didn't get them . .

My first reason to visit Maine – a visit that in short order would lead us to buying a piece of a Maine island and building Moosewood – was to do a TV profile on an upcoming young writer. Appropriately, therefore, I had recently purchased one of his latest books, a volume of short stories. That should satisfy our horror hungry campers, a lamplight reading of a Stephen King tale titled *Lawnmower Man.*

And? By the time that reading was over, Mary Jo had left the room, I wished I had, and the kids were hollering for more.

Instead, we happily decreed it was time for evening prayers. The girls, whatever year it was and whichever girls they were, were Christians, being brought up in families of faith and prayer but, perhaps, not the kind of prayer we introduced them to. Put simply: we put it simply.

We did not recite memorized, ritualistic prayers. You might say we didn't so much pray as just sit there talking to God. Asking him questions, recounting our blessings that day and saying how grateful we were. Then, one by one, we'd ask the campers to remember and thank. That done we'd sing a verse of a hymn they might know even if only God Bless America. And it was off to bed, a God-blessed day ended and gratitude expressed. Ready for tomorrow.

Daytimes, the campers explored, hiked the island, scrabbled down to the shore to seek "lucky rocks," our dogs trotting along with them and, of course, the girls' whistles hanging securely around their necks. At first, one of them was much more skittish scrambling the rocks down by the sea, unsure of her footing and always hanging back timorously. Slowly though, with our encouragement and the modeling of her friend, she gained confidence and soon was hopping happily rock to rock, unafraid. Until . . .

Her dad dropped in from a business trip to see how the kids were doing and suddenly the girl who had overcome her fears scrambling seaside rocks, relapsed. *"Dad?"* And dad came to help her do what she had been doing by herself for several days. Each of us – a child especially – is a different person when among different persons. It was good, we thought, that "Dad" had to leave the next day.

Each day at camp, time was allocated for classes – crafts and nature. Clustered around our picnic table out on the porch the girls would listen to Jo's teaching about trees, deciduous and coniferous, sending her pupils out quickly to gather samples of each. She'd teach them how to distinguish the conifers by counting the needles in each bundle. She taught them how to tell by aroma which of the branches she brought forth was balsam fir, and then helped each of them use fir clippings to stuff a small aromatic pillow to present to their parents as they returned home.

Indeed, at one year's camp session, the girls wanted to know more about sewing. Their first stop on their first day, thus, was to be taken to a sewing store in a neighboring town to select patterns and fabric and thread, buttons, needles and pins. Then back to Moosewood to begin their classes. This, too, was something they had never been allowed to do back home. But both of that year's campers took to it enthusiastically such that by the time camp was ended, they flew home and their parents greeting them at Los Angeles airport were surprised to see each girl proudly wearing a complete new outfit that she herself had made.

That was surely the highlight for that year, but every year the important focus for the kids – we made sure – was nature. A friend of ours, a park ranger, Meg Scheid had written and illustrated a charming children's book called *Discovering Acadia / A Guide for Young Naturalists*. It became our pupil's text and test book each year at Camp Moosewood.

Fill a plastic container with seawater and put into it a sample creature from a tide pool so it can be observed from all sides and

underneath as well. If barnacles on rocks are uncovered, swish seawater on and around them and watch them come out to feed. Learn
how dog whelks eat barnacles, their favorite food. Learn how you can
eat seaweed, like the red-purple dulse you can pick up at the shore
and it's good for you. Learn not to touch the needle sharp spines of
sea urchins, covering their globular shells. Learn too that once the
sea urchin dies and its spines have fallen away, you can see a marvelous miniature light show looking upward through sun-prick patterns
in perfect geometry on the empty shell. Learn how raccoons have
mirror-like structures in their eyes to intensify light so they can see
so well in the dark. Those mirrors also make the animal's eyes shine
bright yellow in beams of flashlights. Learn that fireflies (not really
flies but beetles) identify each other during mating by the timing and
color of their signal lights.

We would head out with our pupils into Acadia to a series of
ponds that had been created by beavers. See first the short, pointed
stumps in the woods surrounding, beaver chewed, each. Then follow along to where the beaver-felled trees were used laboriously to
build the dams that would turn a flowing creek into a lake in which
the beavers, working communally, had constructed their lodge,
its entrance underwater to forestall predators. Clever guys those
beavers!

Back home, the girls could see the small table we had made with
smaller beaver-chawed logs for legs and it would mean something to
them it hadn't before. The one thing I denied them was to read the
little poem I had written about beavers and their dams. It appeared
in my first book of Poetography but might not be – as they say – age-
appropriate for our tender campers.

> Dam! *Say the beavers, ambitiously clever*
> *Wanting the water as moat for their den*
> Damn! *Say the people at such endeavor*
> *Wanting no pond where a pond hasn't been*

So beavers at the water-gate
Weave wondrous walls of limbs and leaves
While sour people derogate
Each behaves as each believes

That's how it goes in life's exam
Some pupils build while some decry
Depends on which they're driven by
The urge to dam
The urge to damn

Our former young campers from Camp Moosewood are grown wom-en now. I don't know what recollections they hold but I treasure many matchless memories. It was a privilege, it is always a blessing to be able to introduce young people more intimately to nature, because, so doing, you are introducing them more intimately to God in His most tangible, touchable form. There's no app for that.

The study of nature, I believe, is as important for a student – young or old – as reading.

Indeed, at times, nature and reading are the same.

READING

I like to read. Enjoyable and worthy are my times spent reading. Nor does reading mean I have to go off alone, sequester myself in a room with a book – even if it be the Book of Books. It doesn't mean I need to power the Kindle or Nook or spin an audiobook though I do those things on occasion. But often, my reading is done in other ways. I mean, there is reading and there is reading.

It is fashionable in glossy magazines and Sunday supplements to compile Best Reading lists – for the beach in summer, the fireplace in winter – lists of the listmakers' own favorite books. Many of my reading preferences will never find their way to those lists. Listmakers would listen to my choices and deem me unhinged.

Well, I am hinged, though my hinge may swing differently than theirs, even your. For example, among the things I most love to read: I love to read water. Have you tried reading water? I recommend it. There are stories to be heard, seen and imagined while reading water. Shouldn't imagination always be a part of reading?

Seaside offers compelling reading. Sometimes, it menaces with angry, lashing waves in full throat cursing the beach with sagas of peril, impending or met. Of ships and sailors lost, the victorious waves then dashing ashore to boast of their conquest. Or perhaps, more frighteningly, to warn of conquests to come. *This island of yours,* they bellow, *what you glibly call your barrier island; do you really think that if we challenge and assault it, your "barrier" will bar?* So taunt the raging waves in this dark and malignant imagining.

Read another piece. The library of imagination is unbound and unbounded. Read whimsy. What you see as you read is the same beachfront but now refined, its waters of placid mien. The characters in the account appear to be four. A small boat a ways offshore holds a single fisherman, conveying him nowhere, bobbing in place while the angler readies his gear. Then, at the shoreline, statuesque and fine, a great blue heron, grateful that his aspect is more becoming than his ill-fitted voice. The last character in the scene is unseen because it is I, both the observer and the reader of this quizzical bit of doggerel.

Fishing

Birds are fishing
Men are fishing
In the water fish are fishing
While I stand wishing, fondly wishing
Not to be a fish!

Not all my reading is jocular, not all profound. (Though I find that that which isn't, sometimes is.)

The water of a stream at the foot of a great mountain flows by my feet and comes to a place where the stream-bed is laced with a line of rocks bringing the water to rippling, bubbling playtime. It braids itself in twisting strands then unbraids and starts to dance, having, it seems, a jolly good time. It deserves it, has earned it. I read how hard water works, doing so much for so many. It floats our boats, it shapes the shore; frozen it scoured mountaintops millennia past so that now we enjoy those rounded hills; pooled, it slakes the thirst of bird and beast; flowing, ferries nourishment; soaking, greens the grasses; gathered, mirrors the beauty of many a beautiful spot. It works so hard that I think it fair, every now and then, it gets a chance to play. Approvingly, I read the waters as they frolic.

Out across west Texas plains, I squint into the distance at the winding coruscation of the Rio Grande. Oh yes, the water of that river, too, has a story for me to read, a story about itself, not just the parts of the river I can see but as well the parts I cannot. The whole thing, from headwaters to gulf to sea. This is a story about a river and, I find, about us all.

Angel Unaware

*The bubbling spring will never know the stream it's bound to
be,*
Nor slipping spring the river that is its destiny;
*To the river up here, the river down there is an unknown
quantity*
And none of those, of course, begins to comprehend the sea.
Curious, is it not, how like are they and we?

We no less are bubbling springs though usually unknowing
Heedless of the spirit waters from us ever flowing
To our friends and everyone we come across, bestowing
Silent witness; teaching not by talking but by showing
Inadvertent testimony everywhere we're going

You are an incognito saint. Where you go today
*Will be people who need your wash of Godness more than they
will say*
*Your spirit can love them, lift them, light them, lead them on
the way*
If you will just remember that the only Jesus they
Have ever seen may be the Jesus they find in you today.

Yes, at times my readings of water do get a bit preachy. Maybe they think I need it. Maybe they're right.

Years ago the great Polish poet and Nobel Laureate Wisława Szymborska composed a poem about water that inspires me still.

It is early on a moist May morning and the water I read this time is but a single drop. I am crossing the meadow at Moosewood when I come upon it. Another month and great stands of colorful lupine, some flowers lavender, some white, some pink, will adorn this part of the field but for now, before the blossoms themselves form, only their palmate leaf fans are deployed. The sun this morning has not yet burned through to dry the dew that is spattered atop the leaves. My focus narrows to one plant on which dewdrops from most of its fourteen leaflets have run down toward the center of the fan, forming a single large dewdrop. That is the subject. That is what I read.

Dewdrop

The lupine this morning embraces a dewdrop
Soon in the sun to dry.
All I know of that drop of dew
Is that It knows more than I.
I know Now, at least a bit,
It knows Now and Then.
It has traveled Everywhere
Lived through Everywhen.

Dipped from a stream by the hand of the Baptist
It moistened the brow of God.
As sweat it cooled the nape of a plowman
Busting Dakota sod.
One day it joined Niagara
Thundering free and wild,
Another, drifted as a flake
To light on the lash of a child.
It plumped the grape that became the toast
To a new life bound together;
It rode the cloud of stormy night,
Fled in sunny weather.

It was the ice that cleft recalcitrant crags,
Frost on April flowers;
Wisława translated its multifold guises
To verse for contemplative hours.
It fell with the rain that nourished the Bo
Beneath which the Buddha found peace.
It rose from the breath of a dinosaur;
It spattered the tattered valise
Of an immigrant newly arrived with a dream
From a land where no dreams were allowed.
It was the tear of a dear young girl,
Loved, left and proud;
(She would not know that not long after
It would be his tear too).
It has been blood and flood and mud
And now, the morning dew.

What next? And where? We cannot know;
That lies beyond our ken.
But that drop of dew knows a thing or two –
Everywhere and Everywhen

There is another form of reading I have taken up. This, I learned from my wife. She taught me to read *sand*, the engrossing stories to be told by a beautiful beachful of sand. If it's the right beach and the right time of year there are indeed telling tales of turtles, sea turtles, long time survivors on this planet but these days, threatened and endangered.

She is a volunteer, licensed by state government to monitor, tabulate and safeguard the sea turtles along a mile-and-a-half long stretch of beach. They are mostly Loggerhead turtles along with occasional Greens and Kemp Ridleys, that come ashore in summer to dig their nests, lay their eggs and found the next generation of their threatened species. The volunteer goes out before sunrise; sometimes, I tag along. Not the water itself this time to read but the tracks in the sand. Those can tell wondrous stories.

I'm lagging. From up the beach, Jo calls: "Got one." I hurry to catch up. What she and her partner have is a set of markings running from the waterline, heading up the sand toward the line of seaside vegetation. Each run of tracks comprises the animal's footprints dug in on either side of a smooth belly drag. (Or, be the turtle a Green, there'll also be the distinct mark of a tail drag). The turtle was heavy – Loggerhead, three or four hundred pounds – not designed for hauling her heft over land, especially when burdened by all the eggs she needed with some urgency to expel. From the footprints themselves, how the sand has been pushed one direction or the other in each print as she lumbered her way, her direction can be told. She wandered and wove a bit heading up the beach, seeking just the right site, a place high enough that waves shouldn't reach the nest once laid, and clear of rock that would interrupt her digging and make her give up and either leave to return another day or wearily trudge to another spot. When finally she finds what she wants she squats and begins digging, scooping the sand with her rear flippers, excavating a hole two feet or more deep. She waddles over, positioning her rear quarters over the nest and goes into a state of fixation nearing trance as she begins depositing her eggs. For most of an hour she will be here dropping eggs into the sand "basket" she created. Each egg is white, leathery, the size of a ping pong ball and she fills her nest with a hundred, a hundred ten, hundred twenty eggs, stacking layer upon layer. In her trancelike state she can hardly be disturbed. Turtle volunteers can cement a transponder onto her back and she'll not know or care.

When finished laying, she comes to and, using her flippers again, covers the nest over with sand and then she leaves, wearily hulking back down the beach to the water to swim away. Her babies are "her babies" no more. She will never see them again or if, by phenomenal coincidence she does, she won't know them. A sea turtle, post-laying, has no further maternal duties or awareness. She goes back to sea perhaps to find another male and create a new brood. If the babies, left behind in their shells in the sand of a beach have anyone looking out for them during their two month hiatus in the nest, it is the God-assigned caretakers called a turtle patrol and in most places, those don't exist.

What she has left in her tracks this morning is the remarkable tale of a persistent, prescient and nature-blessed mother. Nor was she a total stranger to this beach. Thirty, maybe thirty-five years ago, she last was here, right on this very beach. Does she remember? In a sense we humans can neither understand or explain, she "remembers" for this is her natal beach, the beach beneath whose sands the egg containing her was laid and she was born, those thirty or thirty-five years ago. How did she get back here? How did she – now with compulsive urgency to herself become a mother turtle – find her way back to her own beach? And why? What impelled her, what compelled her? To say nothing of the astonishing navigational instinct that permitted her. I couldn't do what she has just done. You couldn't do it, unaided, by yourself, with no GPS or radar or sonar or sextant. We couldn't do it. She could and did. Dumb animal?

When she left here she was a hatchling, size of a silver dollar (there were such things then), now a three-hundred-fifty pound log-gerhead turtle, mother-to-be. What stories this marine explorer has to tell but in her silence, one must yet again fire imagination. From transponder trackings we know that turtles from this beach travel hundreds, even thousands of miles. From the Gulf coast of Florida as far as the Bahamas, all the way down to the Yucatan. Years ago one of the turtle transponders made it appear that the animal was miles inland in the state of Alabama. How had she gotten there? Hurricane Katrina waters had washed her that far astray before, eventually, pulling her safely back into the Gulf proper. Safe so that when her time comes again, decades later, she can return to fulfill her urgent duty on her natal beach. I would love to be here to greet her.

I suspect that not many people – poetic or prosaic – share my habit of reading either sand or water (not unhinged, they!) but many may share with me another distinctive form of reading.

Lie on your back and gaze. See the pale orange that tinges the cap of cloud on morning's sunrise. It is the bank of seeming snow-capped peaks rising from a tropical horizon. It is the menace of darkling grotesqueries as storms impend. Or, more placidly, it is the parade of puffs that scud and shape-shift across a dreamy sky – an ever-changing, bright menagerie. Read Clouds.

By day the LORD went ahead of them in a pillar of cloud to guide them...

Sky-decorators, givers of shade, bringers of rain, flingers of fire, aerial Rorschach tests – all these are clouds and more.

While Aaron was speaking to the whole Israelite community, they looked toward the desert, and there was the glory of the LORD appearing in the cloud.

Clouds are the answers to questions unasked, questions I ought to put, answers I need to reach and grasp and embrace but how can I? Answer-clouds are vaporous, elusive, evanescent. I can no more clutch a cloud than stay it on its certain, sailing way.

"Look, he is coming with the clouds and every eye will see him. . .

I think of the words in Psalm 18: "The Lord is my rock"

But the rock I read this morning is high and mostly white, set against the blue of early sky. It towers, my rock, but also it moves, ever-shifting, re-forming. I can not reach my rock; I cannot reach my Lord.

I cannot touch my rock; I cannot touch my Lord.

I cannot always see my rock; I never see my Lord. But he is always my Lord, my rock.

Amen.

THE DOCTOR WHO NEVER PREACHED

Let me return to the conventional notion of reading. Specifically to a man who gave readers more wisdom and joy than any nature writer before or since.

"Nature Writer?"

I have mentioned many of the pantheon of nature writers in these pages — Thoreau, Emerson, Lopez, Muir, Abbey, Berry, Dillard, Leopold — but there is one too easy to overlook, to neglect although by some measures he may have been the most effectual nature writer of all. We do not think of him as such but I believe the label is apt. I didn't always. I wasn't thinking of him as a nature writer when I first met him. In truth, when I first met him, I didn't know him. (It is with no small shame I admit that, but then one of the things he taught was that we needn't feel shame.)

Years ago, it was. I was traveling with a group of NBC correspondents for a year-end speaking tour across the country, the sort of thing we did to show the network flag in the hinterlands and, within our small group, try to outdo each other with our dazzles of brilliance and profound powers of perception. We were not humble folk.

This year, the tour came to San Diego and at the end of that performance, I saw a man approach the apron of the stage toward me — a lean, erect fellow, not at all stooped by the seventy or so years he was carrying. I went down to greet him. He spoke softly, complimenting me on my ideas and expressions. He was nothing but polite, and yet as we talked for a few minutes, I could not help but notice a distinct, even mischievous twinkling in his eyes. That should have been a tip off. That plus his craggy and wonderfully expressive face, which seemed so familiar yet elusive. Mocking sneers and delicious gleams of delight hid just beneath the surface as this man, this elderly Mr. Geisel, he said, spoke with me for several minutes and then turned and left. And I didn't know whom I had met.

When, finally, I realized who Ted Geisel was, I knew why his face held secrets. I had read *The Cat In The Hat* and seen the cat's delicious grin. I knew the Grinch and his mocking sneers. All those and more lurked in the crags of the face of Theodore Seuss Geisel – *Dr. Seuss!*

The frustration of having met an idol without realizing it persuaded me somehow to meet him again. Actually, it shouldn't be hard, should it? I would simply offer to do a TV story about him. Simple.

Not simple. The first time my producer and I made the approach – properly, formally, through public relations and publishing people, we struck out. "Sorry," we were told, "he doesn't do TV. Not at all. Never." I tried again using various other approaches, but eventually, disappointed but admiring this man's determination, I gave up.

A few years later a producer named Beth Polson came along whose second greatest professional talent was doing the undoable. (Her first was allowing pictures, rather than a superfluous overlay of words, to tell stories.) "Beth," I teased her, "You know what we ought to do? A story on Dr. Seuss. Everyone loves him, but he's never done TV. We've tried. He absolutely refuses. Nobody can get him. Nobody."

Which was all Beth needed.

It took her six months. For the impossible, that's not bad.

First came a simple if limited invitation to his home and studio in La Jolla, California. The limitation was our understanding that we were not coming to do an interview, not that at all. If, after we met each other and he agreed we might later be asked back to do video around the place, watching him work, but that was all. We needed understand that.

He met us at the door of a house he might have created. Clearly the work of a playful, irreverent imagination. Built around an ancient lookout tower, it blended antique Spanish-Mexican solidity with modernist free-spanning glass walls to showcase views of the Pacific. Inside, he displayed many treasures, though none of them the multitudinous Emmys or Oscars he had won. Instead, at the entrance into his studio where so many bizarre creatures were born, there was on a wall a stuffed animal of his own devising. Mounted on a wooden plaque as if it were a hunting trophy, it was a curious, twinkling creature with a stump of bristle rising from its head and a damnably knowing curlicue smirk on its lips.

"A Tufted Guzzard," Geisel said smiling an identical smile. "I never throw anything away."

Which didn't make sense and wasn't supposed to. Not yet. Sense doesn't happen in the first pages of a Dr. Seuss book.

"When I changed from wet shaving to an electric razor," he explained, "I couldn't bring myself to throw away the old brush." The Tuft of the Guzzard.

On another wall was a Stuffed Ormie. On another, a strangely framed paper target from a rifle range with a good, close cluster of holes, and standing beneath it, the ancient muzzle-loader his dad had used to make them. "He'd practice for hours and hours, determined to become the world's champion. '*Strive for Perfection*,' dad always told me. I keep it to remind me."

Inside his workroom, corkboard walls were covered with storyboard drawings for new projects – here a TV show, there a new book. A low drafting table stood before a wall of windows that looked across the garden to the ocean: a wonderful distraction for the daydreamer, but Ted Geisel, certainly a daydreamer, found more compelling distraction in the squiggles that flowed from his colored pencils. Creatures appeared. He didn't know who they were when he started drawing them, but when they began meeting each other, romping, tussling or bobbly-wussling, then he could identify them. "It's simple. If you find you've drawn a Lorax, you know it's a Lorax. And a Sneetch couldn't be anything else but a Sneetch." From a Doctor named Seuss that made sense.

Mostly, he made sense. Isn't that why he was so singularly successful – more than a hundred million Dr. Seuss books sold, plus some by Theo LeSieg (try it backwards), the name he used when someone else did the drawings. He didn't talk down to kids. He didn't even talk down to parents. And he didn't give them just fluff or whimsy.

"Not whimsy, but satire," he insisted.

"And the difference?"

"Whimsy's the gingerbread business. Lace and frills."

"And satire?"

"Is looking at the world through the wrong end of the telescope."

There were values in his works, values and truths. Spoken through the mouths of anapestic animals.

"I never preach," he said, "but my characters do."

They preach tolerance, urge us to realize that for every Us there is a Them who may be smaller and need our forbearance, or larger and deserve our humility. They tell us that language is a gift we should treasure by using it, playing with it. They teach in the most effective way one can teach either child or adult – by entertaining.

The genius behind those characters was *behind* those characters for a reason: without them, he was painfully shy. "I'm sorry, I really am, but I just can't do an interview for you. Whatever else you'd like, fine, but please don't ask more. Not for television."

We could photograph him working, talking with children, signing books, meeting admirers — but no interview. Please.

Said his wife, Audrey, "You may not think that's much, but it's more than anyone else has ever had."

How could that be?

She offered thoughts. When he was very young, Ted Geisel was a German brewmaster's son in Springfield, Massachusetts, roughly the time of the first World War and prohibition. Wasn't it natural that other kids (who's crueler than kids?) would nickname him "The Drunken Kaiser?" That hurt.

Then, on top of that: young Ted had earned a Boy Scout award and the president of the United States, Theodore Roosevelt, happened to be in town and was enlisted to present the awards to the scouts. As the president dutifully called off the names of the winners, he missed one name, ignoring Ted completely. Noticing one boy unacknowledged the president asked about him and was told, "Never mind; he's nobody." And Ted heard that. And would never forget. And maybe that was the moment something in him decided never again to allow anyone to put him in such an exposed and public position to be humiliated.

Even the name Dr. Seuss was a way of hiding. Realizing that he was unlikely to ever be awarded a doctorate, he gave one to himself, adding it to his Germanic middle name whose pronunciation, for the purpose, he Americanized from *soyce* to *soose*.

Today's readers of Dr. Seuss books would be mystified to see the name on insecticide advertisements from decades earlier. But that's how Ted Geisel started, as a commercial artist, for seventeen years drawing his curious characters for the Standard Oil product called "Flit." As he recalled later, those ads ("Quick, Henry, the Flit!") became the longest-running campaign in advertising history. Toward the end of the series, mosquitoes were driving tanks and piloting Zero-like dive bombers because, by then, it was World War Two.

"Only good thing about the war," recalled Geisel, "it got me out of drawing those ads."

Should you go to the Special Collections Library at U.C.L.A. and dig out those old originals, you will not only smile at the familiar whimsy but be amazed at how, even then, before Dr. Seuss was writing Dr. Seuss books, he was drawing Dr. Seuss characters.

Escaping a career of selling Flit, he went into Frank Capra's U.S. Army movie-making unit. So add this curious distinction to the achievements of Theodore Seuss Geisel: He won three Academy Awards. One was for Best Documentary Short in 1946, a film called "Hitler Lives." Later, another Oscar winner: "Design for Death," a history of Japan. His third win was a non-military production, the cute little animated short "Gerald McBoing-Boing."

It was back while he was still in advertising that he became an author. He wrote a little children's book titled *The 500 Hats of Bartholemew Cubbins*, and the twenty-eighth publisher he sent it to decided to take a chance. That was the start. The books kept coming. Sometimes the message was only that it's fun to read — but that was message enough. Dr. Seuss taught generations of children to love books while giving us stories that unfailingly pleased us and more often than not taught us more than we knew we were learning.

When Horton heard a Who, he gave us more cause to question our own assumptions of superiority or inferiority in this universe than had generations of philosophers – if only because most of us who need to question our assumptions don't read philosophers.

Yertle the Turtle — Oh Marvelous Me, For I Am The Ruler Of All That I See — was his take on Hitler. Shouldn't children be warned from the start against megalomaniacs?

The Lorax told kids (and the grownups reading to the kids) to treasure our earth and all that grows from it and lives on it. It told what happened in the land of the Truffula trees when a queer and greedy fellow called a Once-ler arrived, invited all his relative Once-lers to join him as he built a factory and began cutting down the trees to harvest their tufts ("much softer than silk") to make into knitted Thneeds, one of which, he claimed, every person needs. Ah, but so great was his avarice and so little his concern for the trees and creatures dependent on them and so polluting his ever-growing factory that before long, everything lively and wholesome and good about the land was despoiled. So that now, it is up to us, us young people to begin the hard work of repairing and replenishing the earth's bounty which greed has well nigh destroyed.

That one story, that one book published back in 1971, followed by a TV show and decades later a feature film, are enough, in my mind, to qualify Ted Geisel as one of the most effective and widely attended nature writers we will ever have.

Who knew?

Who knew much at all about this timorous, private man? Even what he looked like? Many had only a vague idea. That became clear to me on the day I arrived at Hudson's department store in Detroit to cover his scheduled appearance there only to find myself quickly surrounded by people eagerly awaiting him and assuming from seeing his posters that I was he. Balding, grey-hair, beard, glasses. Made sense. Even the store's public relations representative made the mistake, coming up to me to tell me where I was supposed to go and what I was supposed to do. As quickly as I could, I disappeared to join my crew and plan our camera angles, leaving the PR gal to locate the actual Ted Geisel.

We were permitted to shoot Geisel's signing books for his fans, adult and children. But wasn't there any way we could get him to answer a few questions, even if he had firmly ruled out an interview? We'd have to see if an opportunity might appear.

Though shy, Geisel was enduringly patient and accommodating. Scheduled to sign for an hour, he signed book after book without complaint for most of three hours. Producer Beth now and then prompted someone in the line to ask the Doctor one of our questions; that got us a few sound bites. As he was signing a copy of his *Marvin K. Mooney Will You Please Go Now?*, a woman asked, "Do people know the other meaning of that book?"

Our camera captured his answer: "I sure don't tell them."

The story-within-the-story was that Ted Geisel had once run into the humorist Art Buchwald, who chided him for not writing a political book though the nation was mired in Watergate. Geisel's response was to take a copy of the little book he'd written two years earlier and cross out the name Marvin K. Mooney each time it appeared, replacing it with Richard M. Nixon. Buchwald printed excerpts of his new version in his column. "Richard M. Nixon *will you please go now!*"

By the end of the afternoon, Ted Geisel was exhausted and finally allowed to step down. Gently we steered him to a corner where he could sit, away from his public, have a soft drink and relax. If he noticed that our camera was set up in that corner, he neither acknowledged it nor objected. I sat down with him and began... certainly not interviewing. *Conversing.* A simple chat between two guys both balding with grey hair, beard and glasses. But in those moments, we captured on film in a completely natural way more of his kindly candor than we could ever use in our story. To be sure, he said, he was grateful there was so much public attention and affection, but he was not and never would be comfortable with it. He wrote what he wrote — simply playful or "playful preaching" because he loved doing it. If it taught, terrific. But that placed upon him a tremendous responsibility — to discern the right things to teach and then teach them in a way that wasn't teaching. Kids or adults for that matter don't want to be "teached at." Won't accept the teachy/preachy.

Such were his gentle and not inconsiderable ramblings there for most of a half hour as he relaxed and unwound.

Of course, he knew exactly what was happening but, not feeling threatened by us, had no problem having conversation even with a camera nearby, watching.

Far as I know, it was the only television interview Dr. Seuss ever did.

That time with him would come back to me years later when I was asked to be the commencement speaker one spring at the University of Maine. Honored though I was, I had no conviction that I possessed any wisdom that young folks coming out off college absolutely had to have. What could I say?

And I remembered that Geisel himself had once been asked to do such an address at Lake Forest College in Illinois. As a shy man, he didn't want to risk such a public spectacle, but Lake Forest was his own alma mater. So he gave his address the only way he could — not as himself but as his famous alter ego.

Here, in it's entirety as I recall it from being told during our research, was Dr. Seuss' very brief commencement address:

My Uncle Terwilliger and the Art of Eating Popovers

My uncle ordered popovers from the restaurant's bill of fare
And when they came, he regarded them with a penetrating stare.
Then he spoke great words of wisdom as he sat there in his chair:
"To eat these things," said my uncle, "you must exercise great care;
You may swallow all that's solid, but you must spit out the air."

Now as you go on through life, that's darn good advice to follow:
Do a lot of spitting out hot air and be careful what you swallow.

That was all. What more was needed?

Subsequently, as I was to be similarly honored in Maine, I stole creatively. To the chagrin of the graduates I began by informing them that I would be delivering not one but two commencement speeches. (GROAN!)

The first, of course, was Geisel's "Terwilliger," verbatim. Followed by:

If the doctor could do it, then why shouldn't I?
A commencement address as a poem.
A few lines of verse – for better or worse
And we all can be on our way ho-em.

So, graduates, what can I tell you? What rules
Of life for you to ignore?
Here are eight. You don't have to listen.
I'm sure that you've heard them before.

#1. Be what you want .. and not
What you think someone thinks you should be.

#2. Life's not a spectator sport.
So for life's sake, turn off the TV.

#3. Break free of the Internet.
Use it. It might save a minute
Or two. But then shut it down.
Please, don't lose yourself in it.

#4 And this might surprise you to hear me
Proclaim such heretical views
But believe me, I've been there, I've done that, I beg you:
Spend less time with The News.
The news is meanness, contention, grotesqueries.
People who lie, cheat and steal.
Turn off the news. Oh, and remember:
Reality shows are not real.

#5. Don't smoke. And no coke
Even what comes from a can.

#6. Trust yourself. If you feel you can do it,
Go to it, you'll find that you can.

#7. Heaven is not where you'll go
When you die in some faraway year.
Heaven's the peace and the joy and the love
That you make right now, right here.

And finally #8. Don't believe what I've said.
Don't believe anyone's spinning
Think for yourself, study, learn,
Your education is only beginning.

AND WHILE I'M PONTIFICATING . . .

Finally, I would like to say what I would like to have said finally. If that seems a palindromic, remember, you were warned at the outset that words in these pages would be encouraged to play.

So I now shall write this brief epilogue about my epitaph, the epitaph I shall never have. To begin with, I am still not persuaded I'll ever die though I hope I will. From all I'm told about what happens next, all I have come to believe, I don't want to miss it. My second reason to doubt I'll have an epitaph is that I intend no grave, no cemetery plot. Ashes for me, please, not marble.

Still, even before I found myself snuggling up against the age one is expected to drool and make morbid, I thought about what one day I should have as my epitaph. What should it say on the headstone I don't intend to have?

A first impulse led me to rehearse the criticism we TV news people heard so often. A person contesting a story we did would try to escape the opprobrium by averring that their words had been shamefully "taken out of context." I heard that so many times I couldn't stop hearing it as I considered my choice of a moot epitaph. How about having the stonemasons simply grave as my ultimate plaint: *Talk about being taken out of context!*

Another possibility occurred to me from the work I was doing, documentaries especially, being recycled again and again. I thought of this for an epitaph: *I'm not really dead; I'm in reruns.*

That was my thinking back when I had a sourly secular view of life. As that mindset got unset I knew a growing awareness and a grateful acceptance of the God who led me through my enlightening years and consummated a lifelong transformation from non-believer to wanna-believer to make-believer to – finally – committed believer. Which carried an obligation. There's one more step in such transformation and that is to follow the instruction from God through his son, Jesus Christ, to carry the word forth to all the world, which is to say, grow from committed believer to *proclaiming* believer. That was the purpose behind my previous book and has been with this. It also led me to select another expression for the epitaph I'll never have.

This one springs not from the world of news but (not far removed) the realm of advertising, in particular, those heinous effronteries called *Infomercials.* The locution seems never to change and whatever the item being hawked, right after the hawker has persuaded the gullible that it's an unbeatable deal just as it is, he sweetens the pot by peremptorily delivering the words I consider the perfect epitaph for me or any Christian believer:

But wait, there's more . . .